Reeducation in Postwar Vietnam

TEXAS A&M UNIVERSITY

75

MILITARY HISTORY SERIES

Reeducation in Postwar Vietnam

Personal Postscripts to Peace

EDWARD P. METZNER

HUYNH VAN CHINH

TRAN VAN PHUC

LE NGUYEN BINH

Texas A&M University Press • College Station

Library of Congress Cataloging-in-Publication Data

Reeducation in postwar Vietnam : personal postcripts
    to peace / Edward P. Metzner . . . [et al.].
        p.   cm.
    Includes index.
    ISBN 1-58544-129-5 (cloth : alk. paper)
    1. Vietnam—Politics and government—1975–
2. Huynh, Van Chinh.   3. Tran, Van Phuc.
4. Le, Nguyen Binh.   5. Political prisoners—
Vietnam.   6. Prisons—Vietnam.   I. Metzner,
Edward P., 1925–   II. Title.
DS559.912 .R43   2001
959.704'4—dc21   2001000224

To the many untold thousands of our former South
Vietnamese allies who did not survive the postwar "peace."
To those who died in the so-called reeducation camps and
those who perished at sea fleeing to where freedom still
beckoned. They all, sadly and tragically, were casualties
of a war whose carnage rightfully should have ceased
on April 30, 1975.

Contents

Part III. Col. Le Nguyen Binh's Story

Part IV. One a Hero, One a Saint

Illustrations

Preface

Twenty-three years ago, in August, 1974, I left the land and people of Vietnam. For seven difficult but rewarding years I had served as a pacification advisor, mostly in the beautiful, deadly, densely populated, and hotly contested villages of the Mekong Delta. Once gone, I tried to put those emotion-filled years behind me. I could not. My involvement in helping a deserving people grasp their wish for freedom had been too long and too intense.

From my first arrival in October, 1964, many friendships had been formed and solidified, with a depth and sincerity that far exceeded the official limits of our relationship as advisor and advised. When America turned its back on the death throes of the Republic of Vietnam in the spring of 1975, I experienced a profound and unrelenting sense of loss and guilt. As an advisor, I had the duty and privilege to work among farmers, merchants, civil servants, and soldiers, starting in humble and remote hamlets and ending at the highest levels of South Vietnamese authority. I trudged countless rice paddies, hamlets, villages, and isolated mud-walled outposts, continually impressed by the common expression of uncommon calm courage and fortitude of the people. Witnessing their hopes, sorrows, and pain, often sharing in them, I was convinced then, and remain so now, that America was engaged in doing a right and honorable thing. The story of those unforgettable years and what made them so special is told in my previous book, *More Than a Soldier's War.*

After years of fruitless hoping and inquiring about the fate of my friends and comrades in arms, total absence of any response convinced me that they had not survived. Many years later, in 1994, unexpectedly and happily, a series of unrelated chance events began that ended up putting me in touch with one, then another, and finally most of those who had made it through the nightmare of Hanoi's vengeance. The joy of our reunions was tempered by the news each brought of others not so fortunate, who were either executed or perished in prison. This book is a follow-up to the first. It tells what happened to the survivors from the time we said farewell until we met again more than two decades later.

When most previous wars ended, soldiers of the losing side were allowed to lay down their weapons and return to families, farms, and previous pursuits. They were permitted to begin reconciliation and the process of putting fragmented lives back together again. Only those who committed crimes against law and civilized conscience were imprisoned and punished. That is not the way it was in Vietnam. Since the malevolent brand of North Vietnamese communism viewed the moral foundations upon which justice and compassion are based as being mutually exclusive to its existence, it inherently followed that Hanoi would use the so-called postwar peace to prey on the helpless, and they did.

On May 3, 1975, just three days after the last Americans were ignominiously plucked by helicopters from the roof of the defunct U.S. Embassy, the Communist Military Management Section issued Order Number One—mandating that the defeated report to and register with the Communist regime—from its new Saigon headquarters, located in what had been the South Vietnamese Armed Forces Joint General Staff compound. Under the pretense of offering clemency and the lure of citizenship in the new society, subordinate Communist headquarters throughout the country quickly issued implementing directives to Order Number One that specified dates and places for the procedure.

The president, vice president, prime minister, senators, and congressmen, all Supreme Court justices, and all senior government agency officials and teachers were targeted for reeducation, the length of which depended on Communist-perceived degrees of guilt against "the people." Military men, especially officers, received more rapid and detailed scrutiny of their service and rank. Generals were to report from May 8 to 9, colonels from May 8 to 11, other grades of officers from May 8 to 14. Noncommissioned officers and private soldiers were similarly grouped and directed. Registration of the entire armed forces, including police officers and civilian employees, was scheduled to be completed before the end of May.

Depending on combined factors of rank and the nature of duty performed—military men detached to civilian government agencies were considered by the Communists to be CIA agents—specified groups were instructed on June 20 to report for "thought reform" with enough papers, pens, clothes, mosquito nets, and food or money to last ten to thirty days. Because most noncommissioned officers and privates, except for those who had served in intelligence, marine, airborne, or ranger units, were released after undergoing only three days of reeducation classes, some commissioned officers and high-ranked civilian government officials vainly hoped to receive similar indulgence. It was not to be. The instructions to prepare for between ten to thirty days of indoctrination was a ruse to forestall incidents of civil disobedience. The truth was that all remaining groups were sent away to so-called reeducation camps in the remote jungle, with no intention or plan to return them until they were no longer considered a threat to the state. In this manner, a conservatively estimated 250,000 people disappeared, the lucky ones for years, the unlucky, forever.

The real war criminals became the jailers of men of good and civilized conscience. For what crimes were they imprisoned and penalized? They were brutalized for comprehending the true meaning and value of freedom and responding to a deep-rooted desire to achieve it. Families left behind suffered their own kind of terror. Through calculated and harsh deprivation and degradation, the old, the ill, women, and children were punished for the wickedness of envisioning and reaching out for a better life for their children.

True to recorded infamous examples of history—such as events behind the Iron Curtain following World War II, in Cambodia during the Pol Pot regime of horror, and occurring everywhere else that despots oppressed behind a protective cover of censorship and secrecy—a steady stream of clever and deceptive propaganda from Hanoi brazenly claimed that nothing heartless or heinous befell the conquered people of South Vietnam.

Each of my former comrades who has contributed to this book has chosen to tell his story so that history and moral record might be set straight and that an accurate presentation of fact will illuminate and distinguish truth from the blatant fabrication and fiction spewed from Hanoi.

Several others whose experiences also belong here are not included for reasons of their own choosing. Mr. Le Van Hoi and I worked together in 1967 in Dinh Tuong Province, he as the deputy province chief for administration and I as the province senior advisor. Later he was the mayor of Rach Gia City, the autonomous capital of Kien Giang Province, during 1970 and 1972 when I again served as province senior advisor.

Mr. Hoi feels that because he was a civilian who "only spent one year in prison," his ordeal is unworthy to be included with others. I cannot agree with that assessment since for years Hoi played an important role, successfully implementing the lesser heralded though no less important aspects of pacification as it related to urban populations.

When Saigon fell, Hoi was then working for the government's National General Directory of Housing, in planning and development. Such an outwardly unimposing position worked to his advantage when the Communists administered their "people's justice," getting him a one-year sentence. Had the Communists known of Hoi's previous record of carrying out the nation-building objectives of the south, he would not have been so fortunate.

Mr. Tran Khuong Trinh, the Vietnam Supreme Court justice who helped my wife and I obtain custody of her children, similarly feels his experiences will add nothing to what he considers the more significant narratives of others. He insists on wishing to remain silent even though his period of "reeducation" lasted eight long years, after which he was prematurely released by the Communists only because they were convinced he was about to die.

Trinh's experiences would have important singular aspects to add because there is no doubt that his extended term of imprisonment was levied for the sole reason that he was an integral part of South Vietnam's system of ethical justice. In the minds of the Communists, such a "misguided" principle was a menace, and those who held, espoused, or administered it required complete reeducation before release. Obstinate cases could expect to wither in prison until death released them from their agony.

One former counterpart whose story is not told here is Col. Nguyen Van Tai. Tai was province chief of Kien Giang and Vinh Binh Provinces in 1970–71, and I was his advisor in both places. As far as I have been able to determine, Tai chose to remain in Saigon after his release from prison.

My attempts to contact him have been unsuccessful, but even had I been able to locate and communicate with him, other prior comrades are convinced that Tai would have remained silent for justifiable fear of punishment.

The voices of others have been forever stilled by death. One was the intrepid Captain Trinh, chief of Kien An District, Kien Giang Province. Trinh was an ethnic Cambodian who remained dedicated to serving the people of his district, undeterred by delayed promotion and other disdain from the Army of the Republic of Vietnam, which considered ethnic Cambodians second-class citizens.

From the enemy's standpoint, Trinh was regarded as a competent and fearless government soldier who never flinched in his loyalty. Not long before the loss of Vietnam, Trinh devised and successfully led a plan to recapture from the VC his old district of Hieu Le, located deep in the forbidding U-Minh Forest. Knowing Trinh could not be reeducated, the VC summarily executed him after capture.

The commander of the Province Reconnaissance Unit in Chuong Thien Province under Le Minh Dao, comprising ex-VC returnees, was quickly dealt the same fate as Trinh. Col. Chung Van Bong, a regimental commander before becoming the province chief of Vinh Binh and Dinh Tuong Provinces, died in a reeducation camp. Many others I served with simply disappeared after capture. For the dead, as well as the living who survived that ordeal, the truth of what really happened in the postscript to "peace" in Vietnam must be told.

Acknowledgments

This book exists because three of my courageous former South Vietnamese comrades in arms agreed that the truth must be told and the historical record set straight. The propaganda spewing from Hanoi were blatant lies intended to cover up the postwar vengeance the Communists imposed on the vanquished.

Certain that recalling their experiences would be a sad and emotionally difficult task, my counterparts wrote of their experiences in Vietnamese in order to assure complete accuracy and give them freedom of expression. I thought the combined translating abilities of my wife and myself would be equal to the task. I was wrong. Too many new words, phrases, and expressions that had come into being were beyond our vocabulary.

After a long and frustrating search, the translation solution miraculously appeared from a totally unexpected source. An American who had never been to Vietnam confidently stated he could do the job. Equally important, he strongly agreed that the stories needed to be told. James Banerian is a rare and uniquely talented person who has become a valued friend.

Jim studied the Vietnamese language at Southern Illinois University at Carbondale from 1975 through 1978. He has translated a number of short stories, articles, songs, and poems, as well as histories of South Vietnamese immigrants. His most important work, though, is not a translation. It is a corrective rebuttal of the flawed accuracy of the PBS series *Vietnam: A Television History,* which aired beginning on October 4, 1983. Jim's definitive work, titled "Losers Are Pirates," takes PBS's skewed accounts of Stanley Karnow's history to task item by distorted item. Jim's enthusiastic agreement to join in another effort to get at the truth therefore came naturally.

Tran Khoung Trinh, a former justice of the Supreme Court of South Vietnam and an old friend, also contributed to ensuring the prose of the book made sense and was accurate. This he was qualified to do because he too underwent a period of "reeducation."

Finally, I'm thankful and indebted to my dear and patient wife, Alina, who supported my lengthy, time-consuming, and urgent need to present the truth.

PART I

Col. Tran Van Phuc's Story

CHAPTER 1

Advisory Days

I initially met Col. Tran Van Phuc on my first assignment to Vietnam in October, 1964. He was the province chief of Dinh Tuong Province, and I was an advisor to the Vietnamese 7th Infantry Division, headquartered in My Tho City, the province capital. Phuc's province was one of four important provinces in the Mekong Delta south of Saigon that comprised the division's tactical area of responsibility.

At that time, we did not often work closely together. Phuc had the vast responsibility of running every aspect of the province's civil government programs as well as leading its large militia forces in providing for the protection of the province's population. My job as psychological warfare (psywar) and pacification advisor to the 7th Division also involved me with the protection and welfare of the people, but only in connection with military operations conducted by the division.

One such action, which was the occasion of my first meeting with Phuc, was a battle to oust a Viet Cong battalion from the area of the village of Ba Dua. In appreciation for the division's efforts to protect them before and during the battle and for Phuc's efforts to care for them when the battle ended, the people of Ba Dua asked the government to stay and retain control of their village, which had suffered physical and economic damage, as well as oppression, during two previous years of Communist occupation. Phuc, as the primary government representative, directed the effort to assist and rebuild Ba Dua, and I assisted the division Psywar and Pacification Section, which was assigned to support Phuc. This occasion and several similar ones gave me the opportunity to know, respect, and admire the man I was later to advise during my next tour.

When I returned to Vietnam in 1967 as the Dinh Tuong Province senior advisor, Phuc and I continued our joint efforts to protect the people and implement civil-military programs to improve their lives. The trust and friendship we shared on my first tour continued to grow, deepen, and so-lidify, culminating in our efforts to assure the successful conduct of his country's first national election. Sadly, that historic day ended in tragedy. Returning after dark to the home station after providing election polling-place security, Phuc's personal bodyguard platoon was ambushed. With heavy hearts, we both carried the blood-soaked and broken bodies of the survivors to the province hospital.

Three months later, I was medically evacuated from the province. Before I was returned to duty, I was replaced in Dinh Tuong by another officer when increased enemy attacks in the province provided an ominous, but then unrecognized, precursor of the coming 1968 Tet countrywide attacks. En route to assignment in another Mekong Delta province after I was re-leased from the hospital, I visited Phuc. The date was December 11, 1967. We stayed up until late that last evening discussing topics and ideas per-taining to the war and his people. When the coffee pot was empty, he qui-etly escorted me to one of the second-floor guest rooms in his official resi-dence and said goodnight.

At 5 A.M., a knock on the door awakened me. After a last breakfast to-gether, we shook hands, wished each other well, and parted, and we did not see or hear from each other for almost three decades. Only then was I to learn of his subsequent ordeal.

CHAPTER 2

Saigon Memories

"Saigon dear! I lost you, as you lost your name." These words from a melancholy song that played on a cassette tape late one evening, far away from my homeland, stirred deep nostalgia in my heart. "Saigon, the beautiful! Oh, Saigon." The thought of Saigon, the Republic of Vietnam's capital, so gracious, so lovely, at one time called "The Pearl of the Orient," evoked so many memories and mixed emotions in me.

Saigon, the place where I greeted life and entered the world with my first cry. The place where I had to interrupt my studies, along with other young men, to join the army and defend our country in a fratricidal war between the north and the south, an ideological war in which one who loved freedom had to fight to save South Vietnam from falling under the Communist yoke.

Saigon, where I had to leave my family and spend thirteen years detained in Communist prisons in North Vietnam. Also, where in 1993, I had the good fortune to depart with my family and fly to America, where we could once again live in liberty.

I hesitate to recall once light-hearted and beautiful Saigon back in those gloomy days of late April, 1975, the days when the south was reddened by both the blood of its defenders and the the descending vengeance of the Communist invaders. At that time, echoes of gunfire from distant battles suddenly changed the peaceful atmosphere of the city. The city's defense was organized into checkpoints and fortified posts manned by forces ready to blunt the enemy's advance, while, simultaneously, a large mass of people were running for their lives, using all means of transportation to escape the shelling and air strikes that most thought were soon to descend upon them. The constant roar of fighter planes that were escorting helicopters loaded with escapees added to the unfamiliar and portentous din.

A twenty-four hour curfew made marketplaces, shops, and restaurants deserted and lifeless. Formerly crowded and busy streets were empty, except for an occasional military or police vehicle. I did my best to appear calm in front of my family, telling my wife and children not to panic and to follow the example of neighbors who were also trying to behave as if everything would be resolved.

The worst of all the worst imaginable things came upon us on April 30, 1975, and turned the lives of the people of South Vietnam upside down. I sadly observed piles of discarded military uniforms and equipment that had been abandoned along roadways by demoralized military who were ordered to surrender. Residents who had evacuated a few days earlier now returned home more deeply anxious and fearful. Without a government, Saigon was in chaos. Rampaging and looting went unpunished. Gone forever was the city's flourishing, carefree, and happy culture.

The graceful and feminine *ao dai* was replaced by the drab *ao ba ba,* the dull, drab pajamas long popular with workers and farmers. Bicycles proliferated and replaced autos and other motorized vehicles. In many places, piles of filthy, foul-smelling trash added to the pollution of the city. Hosts of poor children rummaged through the piles in search of anything of value. Some children climbed onto an abandoned armored vehicle about four hundred meters from my house and accidently fired the machine gun. Luckily, the blast caused more panic than damage.

Business activity was slow and dwindling. Markets were devoid of customers, and small grocery stores peddled what little they had left to clients seeking necessities certain to become scarce in the tense and uncertain days to follow. My wife and our next-door neighbor were able to locate and obtain some rice, dried fish, preserved eggs, and fish sauce, about a one month's supply.

I hid my anxiety and concern from my wife and children, knowing that it would not be much longer before we would learn of our fate. Each day, I listened to the former government radio station, now in new hands. Within two weeks, an official Communist communique was repeatedly broadcast, giving the dates and places for persons subject to reeducation to report. I now quietly resigned myself to my fate and prepared to turn myself in.

Soon thereafter, a man in civilian clothes, who spoke in the northern accent and was escorted by two teenage bodyguards, came to ask me if I was Colonel Phuc. I answered yes and invited him to come into the house and sit. As he did, the bodyguards also entered and remained by his side. My visitor asked me if I worked at the headquarters of the Joint General Staff, and I said that I did, serving in the administrative branch. "A district chief?" he inquired. "No," I replied, "I was assigned to the office in Saigon."

Before leaving, he looked around the room. Noticing that the now required photo of Ho Chi Minh was on the wall, he seemed satisfied and stepped out into the front yard. Pointing to the house across the street, he asked if it was the residence of Colonel H., who also was assigned to the Joint General Staff. When I nodded yes, he reminded me to turn myself in on time, then went to the other house. After knocking on the door for a few minutes, it was obvious that nobody was home, so he left.

I guessed that my visitor got information about me and my location from someone in the neighborhood. Since this was my first contact with a cadre of the revolutionary movement, and since he seemed like a decent and well-mannered person, showing no signs of an arrogant victor, this first impression calmed me down somewhat and lessened my fear of vengeance and retribution.

Turning Myself In

Three weeks later, at the end of May, the day came for me to turn myself in. Wearing a short-sleeved shirt, dark colored pants, and sandals, I left home for the first time since April 30. Slowly, I pedaled my bicycle to the announced reporting place, the former House of Representatives of the Republic of Vietnam, in downtown Saigon. The bicycle was an expensive one, a gift from my father, long ago given as a reward when I passed the admission examination to high school with excellent grades. The bicycle had been recently restored and, with the addition of new tires, looked like new. My beloved father, who had cherished his children, had passed away five years earlier. What a pity, I thought, that I probably would soon lose my dearest souvenir from him.

I had arrived fifteen minutes early, yet hundreds of people were already there ahead of me. We were invited inside, where a cadre ordered us to surrender all arms and military equipment issued by our former, defeated government. Another cadre told us to turn in all personal papers, such as identification cards and military cards. We then had to fill out a lengthy questionnaire detailing our personal history and past activities from 1945 to April 30. Most finished the questionnaire in about half an hour, but it took me a little longer because of my long service and many assignments. When I left, about ten people were still writing. A cadre gave me a receipt for the questionnaire, which would also serve as temporary proof of identification and a safe-conduct pass. I cautiously put the receipt in my pocket and left with a sigh of relief. As I quickly pedaled my way back home, my second contact with "revolutionaries" served to further lessen my apprehension about the form and severity of reeducation. Although it was far past lunchtime when I got home, my family had waited on me. After I briefly recounted what happened, everyone felt less anxious, and we began lunch.

Six weeks after the black day of April 30, I still hadn't heard more about what I was supposed to do, or what would happen to me. My first and foremost concern now was for my wife and young children, who I knew would suffer without my presence and support. Finally, the expected second radio broadcast came. All the "fake" military and government officials and reactionary political party members were ordered to report for reeducation. Times and places were given for each category and rank. Specific instructions emphasized that we were to bring personal belongings and enough money to pay for food for one month.

There was a three-day period in which I could report. I felt it would be best to go early since each day I remained at home now would be a day of worry and extreme anxiety for my entire family. I decided to turn myself in on the first day, even though it would be Friday the thirteenth, a day considered an ill omen. After a farewell lunch, my eldest daughter gave me a ride on her Honda motor scooter to the place of assembly designated for processing. It was a girls' high school. We arrived at 5 P.M., and the front yard was filled with those reporting for reeducation, their relatives, and curious onlookers. I got in line with my backpack, then turned to wave goodbye to my daughter while managing a strained smile. About two hundred persons gathered inside, and we were assigned sleeping places in the upstairs classrooms. After we cleaned our assigned area, spread our sedge mats for sleeping, and hung our mosquito nets, I talked to neighbors and asked for news of missing friends. Before going to bed, I inquired about the backgrounds and circumstances of my new acquaintances. I couldn't sleep, tossing and turning until late into the night. I pondered the dim hope we were all nurturing of possibly returning home after only one month of reeducation, a hope raised by the order to bring with us a month's boarding fee.

About fifty people came to report on the second day, and about ten on the third. On the afternoon of the third day, a cadre came to inspect our living arrangement and told us to surrender anything pointed or sharp, such as knives, scissors, forks, nail clippers, and razor blades. We were told we were free to sleep and awake anytime and were permitted to move freely about the school enclosure, but were forbidden to attempt any contact with people on the outside. Meals were prepared and served twice a day by big restaurants in the city. Someone even made a joke that the promise of a one-month course of political instruction with such good food would not be so bad after all.

Going on an Operation

This uneventful period changed abruptly four days later. Around 8 P.M., while many of us were pacing in the fresh evening air of the school yard, the order was given for all to get ready to go on an "operation." This was the first time I heard this word used in this manner, but it wouldn't be the last. It meant a mass movement of undisclosed purpose or destination. At 10 P.M., we were lined up in ranks, and group roll calls were taken. Near 11 P.M., we were led out the main entrance to where buses waited with their windows covered with white cloth. The buses were the commercial kind previously used to transport passengers between the capital and distant provinces. Each had a crew of driver and fare collector/baggage handler. Before boarding, we were cautioned not to cause any disturbance, converse loudly, or talk to the bus crew.

The convoy started rolling along deserted streets after midnight, our way led by a jeep. Another military vehicle secured the rear. Silently observing the direction of travel, I was concerned about and contemplating our fate. We seemed to be going eastward, but to what destination? The young crewman on the bus was kind enough to volunteer that our destination was Long Thanh. The convoy leader in the jeep seemed confused and was leading the convoy astray, either on purpose or from ignorance. After finally returning to the correct route, we arrived at the village of Long Thanh at about 4 A.M. Directed into rows of barrack buildings that had previously housed abandoned orphans, we set our mats on the floor by the light of matches, then, thoroughly exhausted, quickly lay down to sleep without taking off our clothes or putting up mosquito nets.

CHAPTER 3

Thirteen Years of "Reeducation"

I left home to report for reeducation on June 13, 1975, and didn't return until February 17, 1988. That absence of twelve years, eight months, and four days is clearly burned into my memory because of the great and constant pain endured during the separation from my family. The first fourteen months were spent in two camps located in what had been South Vietnam, the remaining eleven and a half years in two camps in the north. With a firm and unshakable faith for seeing a better future, I persevered in overcoming all obstacles and surviving every physical and emotional trial.

Long Thanh Camp

Formerly called Long Thanh Orphan Village, this camp was composed of a group of buildings where orphans of the war were cared for and educated. At the time of our arrival, everything in the camp had severely deteriorated. Doors were missing, tiles were gone, sewage lines were not working, and high weeds covered every open space.

Our first night's troubled sleep was interrupted at dawn by the crowing of a cock. It took a moment for us to realize our situation as we stared at each other, still shaken by the previous night's "operation" that had brought us here. Joining men and women from a distant barrack who were running toward a water reservoir, I recognized some. While washing my face, I learned they'd arrived some days earlier, from a number of collection points throughout Saigon. Moments later, a cadre arrived to give instructions and rules for our activities. There would be two meals a day provided by a private contractor, at 10 A.M. and 4 P.M. Surprisingly, the meals were good. A large water container was to be kept full for bathing and laundering. Our communal toilet was a hole in the ground with boards arranged for seats in semibooths. After the first several weeks, a private contractor was permitted to open a canteen to sell food to us. The small canteen also served as a barbershop.

During this initial period, the routine was slow and without physical or mental pressures. After physical exercise periods at dawn, we spent several hours each day learning revolutionary songs. We were free the remaining time to converse at the canteen or visit other barracks. The favorite late afternoon place was the road from the main gate to the compound center. We called the road "Sunset Boulevard," which was crowded with anxious small groups slowly walking back and forth, talking about anything and everything in order to pass the time and in an attempt to adjust to our new communal life.

The most memorable and heartrending sight of this wistful daily promenade was that of two old friends, one blind and leaning on the other, who led him along while hobbling on one leg. As they hopped and stumbled along far behind the others, their bearing and demeanor reflected dignity and an inner pride for having served as high-ranking officers in the Republic of Vietnam Armed Forces.

Now and then, we longingly glanced at the traffic passing on the nearby highway and momentarily let our thoughts stray to families as we continued to walk until dark. Often, we had to run for cover as a sudden shower broke. When the rain came, so did more and deeper gloom as we were forced to stay inside contemplating the falling raindrops. Frequently, we dashed out into the rain to get a needed, cleansing, open-air shower.

Two months passed without any education taking place and with no payment taken from us for our board. To our questions, we received the response that we would be educated when the cadre was ready to do it. Until that time, most of us hopefully thought that the order to bring enough money for one month's boarding meant that our education would only last a month. As time passed and our doubts grew, the cadre's response was to keep us too busy to dwell on it. For the second time, we were given forms to declare our personal situations and detail our past activities. This time, our declarations had to be written in much greater detail. Using our backpacks or the floor to write on, our backs ached and our muscles strained to complete the task within the short given time.

When the declarations were finished, we were made to clear the compound of weeds. Only a few tools were available, so hundreds of detainees used our hands to clear large areas in a short period of time. When we completed the weeding, we understood the cadre's larger objective in giving us the task. We were told that surely we could see that hard work had made the compound cleaner during the past several days. We must now realize that labor will be a necessary part of the remaining days of our lives. From now on, we would have to work much harder, for only by labor could we cleanse and improve ourselves. Shortly thereafter, we were told to prepare to attend class.

Our classroom was spacious enough, full of benches but no desks. One small desk and chair were at the head of the room for the lecturer. Two shifts alternated attending class, studying such subjects as "Labor Is Glory," "U.S. Imperialists Were the Invaders," and "False Military Men and False Government Officials Were the Slaves of U.S. Imperialists." Each subject was studied for fifteen to twenty days. After each session, an evaluation class was held in which we had to answer questions from the lecturer. Each of us then had to write our thoughts reconstructing our "wrongdoings" in regard to the revolution.

As could be expected, detainees had no rights at all. We had to agree completely with the propaganda being fed to us or receive the lecturer's insults, threats, or worse. A case in point is what happened to one of our classmates, T. V. T. He was a renowned lawyer, a former senator and deputy prime minister of the Republic of Vietnam. During one evaluation session, the lecturer kept berating us as puppets, instruments of the Americans and antirevolutionists who acted against our own people, having no nation, and so forth. As the lecturer became more aggressive and abusive, he singled out T. V. T. as a worst-case example. T. raised his hand for permission to respond, but the lecturer ignored him. T. finally stood up and asked to please be permitted to respond. The lecturer slammed his hand on the desk and shouted to T. to sit down. Security guards then roughly hustled T. out of the classroom.

One Sunday afternoon later, as we were doing our laundry in the courtyard, a large number of armed cadres suddenly rushed in and ordered us to return to our rooms. After conducting a thorough search, they arrested one of us and took him away in a jeep. Later, they announced that the criminal was affiliated with an antirevolution organization just uncovered in Saigon. None of us was able to find out if that was the real reason for the arrest or what eventually happened to the suspect.

About four months into our imprisonment, a cadre came one evening after dinner and searched each room. When finished, about 150 names were called out, mine included, and we were told to get ready for an "operation."

In the noise and haste of preparing, we wondered aloud to each other where they could be sending us.

We boarded unmarked buses at the main entrance, and, after roll call, the convoy departed at 8 P.M., going in the direction of Saigon. A distance before reaching the city, we turned off on Thu Duc Road, arriving at the district prison after 9 P.M. After we were taken to our rooms, a guard came, took roll call again, then abruptly left, slamming shut and locking the door behind him. Fifteen of us in the room stared gloomily at each other under the one bright, dazzling electric light, contemplating our new circumstances.

Thu Duc Camp

Crowded in tightly together and locked behind prison doors, we now clearly understood our status. Thu Duc Camp was run by the Party Security Branch, not by the army, as was Long Thanh Camp, and our lives were to change accordingly. Now, imprisonment accompanied reeducation. In the weeks that followed, more detainees arrived from Long Thanh, filling up the rooms of our prison. One new arrival was kept separate. She had been a major in the police forces.

Our prison, named Thu Duc Center for Reeducation, was in fair condition. We had electric power, running water, and indoor toilets and bathrooms not far from our sleeping quarters. Our eating area was an open, partly covered veranda with long rows of tables and benches that doubled as a reading and writing area. The prison was partitioned into zones by the existing walls and newly added barbed-wire fences. My zone included a cement statue of Buddha, which was destroyed soon after our arrival. The structure that contained it was then turned into a workplace for an educational cadre (EC) to conduct one-on-one interviews with inmates. Another zone contained a statue of Jesus, which stood among various unrelated and discarded items from the previous government. Whether or not the statue was purposely so ignominiously placed, the message given was clear. Religion and Communist atheism could not coexist.

We were organized into cells of ten people. Three cells were organized into a company with an assigned leader to monitor all company activity. Each company was under the direction of a security agent who acted as cadre in charge of education. As before, there were two meals a day. At first, there was sufficient food, but as time went on, the quantity was reduced more and more.

Awakened at 6 A.M. by the clanging of an old shell casing used as a gong, we had fifteen minutes for physical exercise and a short time to clean up before labor or study, which were conducted from 8 to 10 A.M. and 2 to 4 P.M. Labor initially included hoeing weeds, collecting garbage, and cleaning sewers, followed soon after by more difficult tasks such as cutting and transporting wood for cooking and carrying bags of cement or rolls of barbed wire. Weekday studies consisted of examining and commenting on selected books and newspapers. Weekends were filled with sessions of self-criticism and criticism of others regarding the implementation of the four criteria of reeducation: (1) thoughts—the need to adopt and apply new thoughts toward the revolution, (2) labor—working hard and relentlessly to cleanse ourselves of old ways, (3) education—seriously undertaking our studies and openly and courageously engaging in self-critique and the criticism of others, and (4) cooperation—strictly abiding by all camp rules and regulations and frankly reporting all our past activities, hiding nothing.

We were always accused by the cadres of lacking sincerity and firmness in our criticisms, which prevented us from achieving early, satisfactory, and acceptable results. For the third time, we had to elaborate in writing all our past activities and involvements, this time in response to a much more detailed and lengthy questionnaire. Most of us had to redo it time and again before it would be graded "satisfactory."

When my turn came for the one-on-one interview with the EC, he took me aside and delved at length into my past. "Why would a military officer be working in the administrative branch? Weren't you really working for the American CIA?" Anything slightly out of the ordinary raised suspicions that CIA activity was involved. Then he changed tactics. "You were awarded many medals. Did you earn them by having fought against the revolution? Explain clearly to me what you did to merit each award." After I carefully explained each, he glared at me for a period of time to show his displeasure before dismissing me.

Tet, our most important holiday was approaching. Traditional celebration of the holiday centered around family reunions, which made anticipation of this year's occasion painful to contemplate. We had now been away from our families for seven months, without any communication at all. In these sad circumstances, we received a surprise from the camp leadership. We would be allowed some small holiday festivities. We also could write our families and tell them that they could send us a gift package for the holidays. Most subsequently received a gift lovingly prepared by our families, which commonly contained traditional Tet foods. More important than receiving the gifts was the knowledge that our families finally received the long-awaited gift of news from us.

On the eve of the New Year, we were given permission to organize traditional entertainment, including old songs and comic skits written and acted by ourselves. The entertainment ended in an atmosphere of rare joy. As we returned to our rooms, which were unlocked for the occasion, thoughts lingered of the comics and their antics, which made both prisoners and guards rock with laughter. When the explosions of firecrackers welcoming the New Year in a nearby town reached us, we were brought back to the somber reality of our fate and wondered where our families were and how they were doing without us.

CHAPTER 4

Moved to North Vietnam

After the brief respite of Tet, camp activity returned to normal for the following seven months. One night, we were awakened by sounds of conversation and activity from a nearby barrack. Looking outside, I saw inmates there busily preparing for going on an immediate "operation" and signaling to us to let us know. A few nights later, a different zone also made the move. Left for last, we mentally and physically prepared for our turn. About ten days following the first move, it was our turn.

Around 11 P.M., we were ordered to depart and received instructions and some unexplained and unusual words of encouragement from the cadres before we were handcuffed in pairs and led to the usual waiting buses. The military-escorted convoy slowly moved through the silent cover of night to Tan Son Nhut Airport. Unloaded onto the tarmac, we huddled together for warmth and dozed until 3 A.M., when the first light of dawn appeared in the sky. Awakened and ordered to move, we filed aboard two former Republic of Vietnam Air Force C-130 aircraft. As I boarded, I momentarily reminisced about how such aircraft previously had carried me on military missions while the crew gallantly defied enemy anti-aircraft fire. We headed north after takeoff for a lengthy flight, not landing until nearly 11 A.M.

A convoy of civilian cars and military trucks awaited us, surrounded by armed guards. A cadre in civilian clothes, later identified as a colonel from the Ministry of the Interior, addressed us. "This is Gia Lam Airport. You are here in the north because of better conditions here for your education, which will permit transforming you into good citizens so you can soon return to your families. You will be transported to camps in the delta, which are the best we have in the north. While you are in the cars, keep order and be silent. People here feel deep hatred for you and may throw stones at you if they know you are in the cars. Because of this, we have covered the windows."

Ha Tay Camp

When the convoy rolled to a stop in the new camp's courtyard, it was past noon. Both sides of the large court were lined with rows of detention barracks. The barracks were separated into zones by high brick walls. The group I was in was directed to the zone near the main entrance. Our barrack was divided into two large sleeping rooms containing two parallel, double-level wooden stalls accommodating sixty people. When necessary later, the capacity was increased to ninety or one hundred by having inmates lie down side by side like sardines. An electric light was kept burning all night to facilitate control by the guards. At one end of the aisle was the toilet, with a wooden bucket for excrement and a ground receptacle to urinate in. Each day, the waste products were taken to fertilize the rice paddies, vegetable gardens, and fish ponds. An eating area with long tables and benches was built next to the barracks. A large yard in front of our barrack served as our assembly point and physical-exercise field. A distance away, a water tower with a brick, circular apron was the bathing and laundry point.

When we settled into our barrack, our handcuffs were finally removed, having been in place since our departure from Thu Duc the previous night. Most of us had cut and bruised wrists. Our new education cadre was a young second lieutenant who directed us to pick up our belongings from the front yard. After allotting our sleeping spaces, he offered hot tea to refresh us. After a short period of relaxation, we were directed to the eating room. The time was 4 P.M., and our first meal at Ha Tay Camp was surprisingly lavish and special, as if it were a welcome for the first contingent of political prisoners from the south. After that, things quickly became very different, with interminable days of long, hard work and severe restrictions on all our other activities.

Day after day, our only diversion from work was having to read propaganda books and newspapers, then being required to comment on them. Two frugal meals were served each day consisting of rice, some boiled vegetables, and salted water. The food was never sufficient to meet our need. Inmate T. V. T., who had previously been humiliated at Long Thanh Camp, continuously paced alone in the front yard, or in the barrack aisle after we were locked in at night. His sad, sullen face and long sighs were taken by many as bad omens for us all. Not long after, he was found unconscious one morning and died before emergency aid could save him. Was his death the result of a stroke or heart attack, or the result of the mental torture and emotional withering at Long Thanh Camp? He was the first political prisoner to die at Ha Tay Camp, and he was buried with a simple tombstone marked "PCM" (*Phan Cach Mang*—antirevolutionist). Three or four years later, his family was notified to come and retrieve his few belongings.

Winter Weather

The weather began getting colder, an occurrence unfamiliar to us southerners. The camp management distributed blankets, but there weren't enough for all. We gave priority to those who had not brought blankets with them. Later, we were given sedge mats and mosquito nets. Finally, we were issued our dark blue prison uniforms bearing the printing "Cai Tao" (reeducation). During the first three months at Ha Tay, other groups of inmates arrived from the south to fill the vacant detention rooms. I eagerly looked for friends and acquaintances from Thu Duc Camp, but found none. I wondered what happened to them.

For work, we were organized into companies of blacksmiths, carpenters, green-vegetable gardeners, farmers, and so on. I was assigned to a carpentry company of about forty individuals. Among us were high-ranking officers, noncommissioned officers, and prior Communist cadres who had turned themselves in to the old government and fought in Province Reconnaissance Units (PRUs). One Regional Forces soldier who had previously served with me was surprised to find me sharing the burdens and trials of imprisonment with him. Our walk to the work area took about fifteen minutes, and we passed various blacksmith shops, brick ovens, and the green vegetable patches and rice paddies of the camp. Prisoners incarcerated for penal offenses worked in a separated work area.

Two months later, another year's end and Tet holiday approached. We were permitted to write our families and request holiday gifts. This was only the second time in nineteen months of separation that communication was permitted. We added our name and company number to preprinted labels our families were to use in sending the packages. But the return address destination on the gift labels was Chi Hoa Reeducation Center in Saigon City. In this way, the Communists deceived our families into believing we were in Chi Hoa Prison instead of in the north.

Slow Starvation

When the three-day period of rest for Tet passed, we unceremoniously returned to our eight-hour workdays. Locked in our barracks each night, we had to study propaganda newspapers and later present our "comments." Over the months, our strength was slowly leaving us. Our two meals a day, consisting of three hundred grams of rice for both meals, some boiled vegetables, and salted water, was not enough to maintain health. Our minimum daily need for rice alone was six hundred grams, additional food not considered. Many times we had to eat rotten rice, spoiled by worms and years in storage. Now and then, the rice was replaced by some manioc, potatoes, corn, *bo bo,* which was a kind of cereal normally fed to cattle or pigs, or boiled rolls of wheat flour. Exhausted by daylong hard labor and plagued by constant hunger and thirst, we resorted to eating rare, unlucky grasshoppers caught and roasted over small fires. Those who worked in the fields were fortunate to have the opportunity to catch and eat frogs, earthworms, and crickets, in addition to some edible wild weeds. Those who worked the rice paddies occasionally found small shrimp and tiny crabs, which were quickly consumed raw before the guards discovered them. It was a sad, uncivilized spectacle of frail, deteriorating bodies seeking any way to survive.

Although we constantly complained about the insufficient food, the camp commander told us we simply needed to get accustomed to our circumstance. He claimed he was eating the same meager ration, was thriving on it, and was healthy and robust, so we really had no cause to complain. It was a sad, unjust, and painful joke that we tried to laugh at, but our health was now steadily and rapidly declining, made worse by being pushed to achieve arbitrarily high production goals and compounded by the changing weather conditions. Trembling hands and shaky, insecure legs were not up to the tasks set before us. Finally, faced with the reality of our condition, camp authorities raised our daily rice ration from three hundred to four hundred grams, still not enough.

Another problem was the complete lack of proper and effective medicines to treat illnesses. In the beginning, the popular but ineffective *xuyen tam lien* was given for all sickness, including flu, coughs, fevers, and headaches. The tiny, dark green, bitter pill was made from the heart *(tam)* of lotus seeds *(lien).* Gradually, but ever so slowly, some modern medicines were used to treat our illnesses. A year later, a flu epidemic ravaged the camp. I was deathly ill for more than a month and received only some common painkillers. Upon seeing my gaunt and pale face, fellow inmates were shocked and astounded. Many died from malnutrition and lack of effective medicines, such as antibiotics. One former police officer died in his sleep and was found the next morning clutching a small piece of boiled flour in his hand. He had saved it from his dinner for a breakfast he never reached. Shortly thereafter, inmate D. K. N., a roommate, died from chronic edema, which had gone untreated for a lengthy period.

After three years of separation from our families, our captors made the decision that our families should become involved in feeding us. We were allowed to write our families every three months and request twenty kilos of "gifts" from them. Our families at last knew the truth of where we were imprisoned. Although we were happy at the prospect of hearing from our families and receiving their packages, neither we nor they received all the mail that was sent, or got on time that which was permitted to be delivered. Inmates many times accidently found undelivered, half-burned letters in the garbage. Many received letters months after they were dated or post-marked. Every piece of mail was censored, and all packages were inspected. Money, foreign magazines, and even salt were confiscated. Some inmates were so hungry that they ate the contents of their packages a day or two after receiving them. One of my roommates immediately punched holes in a can of condensed milk and emptied the contents in one, long gulp. He then filled the can with water and drained it dry again. Another took great pleasure in slowly sucking the contents of a tube of toothpaste. Yet another poor soul ate a kilo of dried sausage in one sitting. All of us constantly craved fats and sweets. On one rare day when dinner included a piece of cake made from steamed flour, I added some of my precious sugar and margarine to it and shared small slices with some friends who had not received packages of their own. It was both a delicious small treat and a tantalizing, sad reminder of a time long ago.

On several yearly big holidays, we were given a bit of meat or fish. Prior to each holiday treat, we had to undergo a so-called general hygiene day. On each such declared day, we were ordered to display all of our belongings in the front yard and remain with them while cadres rushed into each barrack and searched them from top to bottom. Other ECs conducted a body search and confiscated whatever items they considered forbidden. Some hygiene days were also the occasion to change and reorganize the composition of our companies, including moving members from one room to another.

Our carpentry company was seldom reshuffled, because of the technical knowledge required for us to complete our given tasks. We made every-thing from furniture to all kinds of wooden ware, and not only for use in the camp, but also to fill orders from outside customers. Ironically, we made the coffin for our former camp commander, who had retired, and, after be-ing bitten by his dog, died from rabies shortly thereafter. Now and then, we had to work on our few holidays to complete scheduled projects, later re-ceiving compensatory time off.

The most difficult and exhausting work was toiling in the rice paddies. During harvest time, all companies had to work at that task to complete the harvest. Under an unrelenting, burning sun, long lines of inmates con-tinually labored to cut rice stems until the clanging of an old mortar shell signaled the end of the workday and time to return to camp. We all then hurried to tie stems heavy with grain into stacks that were carried back to camp in two baskets suspended from a shoulder pole. The return route was rugged and slippery and would have been difficult to traverse even without the heavy loads we balanced. Slips and spills were common, and on one of my tumbles I badly sprained my ankle.

After harvest, our labor turned to preparing the paddies for reseeding. The thick, heavy soil had to be turned over, a feat accomplished by water buffalo and inmates. When the rice plants reached a certain height, we weeded the paddies by walking between the rows of rice through leach-filled water and pushing all weeds deep into the mud with our feet and hands. The most-dreaded experience for me was planting the winter-spring rice crop. None of us from the south were accustomed to the freezing cold of the harsh winters of the north and the pain and numbness of sloshing through the icy mud. A second period of pain returned when the numb-ness later left. Trying simply to separate large bunches of rice plants into groups of three stems for hand planting with frozen fingers was next to impossible. Still, I had to push myself through the pain and exhaustion to finish the job as ordered, or suffer the immediate ire of the cadre.

When our farming duties were at last completed, we returned to our ori-ginal tasks and work schedules. At this time, a most disturbing, cruel, and stressful procedure was inflicted upon us by the prison command authori-ties. Selected inmates were exposed to concentrated, intensive, and mind-numbing "education" by special cadres. These unfortunate individuals, who were chosen for this more severe and deep investigation and interrogation because of the nature of their relationships with our former government, were plucked from our midst during midnight invasions of our rooms by camp cadres. All in the room froze and tensely awaited the calling out of the name of the ill-fated victim, who was then taken away to an unknown destination with all belongings.

Most of these unfortunate victims previously had worked for intelligence services, security agencies, or the police forces. The resulting hidden and uninterrupted interrogations lasted several or more days, after which those who underwent them were returned dazed, silent, and uncommunicative. The only evidence of the distress they suffered were the occasional unrepressed moans, which punctuated long periods of silent, detached anguish.

Visit and Feed Policy

After four years of imprisonment, the year-old policy allowing families to "feed" their member-inmates by sending them packages of food was replaced with a "visit and feed" policy. Twice a year, with no limitation on the amount of food that could be brought, families could come to visit us. One afternoon while I was at the workshop, I was informed that there was a visitor who wished to see me. To my extreme shock and happiness, it was my wife. Accompanied by a neighbor friend, she had traveled from south to north by train for three days and nights. After four years of separation and her arduous, anxious, and hopeful travel, a visit of one hour was permitted.

Once we were finally face to face, she could not contain her tears. Seeing me in prison clothes, with my cheeks sunken and dark, and walking slowly and feebly on feet swollen by beriberi, she could not keep control of her emotions; her resolve was stripped away. The cadre controlling the visitation area immediately scolded her for crying. "You are permitted to visit your husband in order to prompt and motivate him to become better re-educated. Why do you cry instead? The next time, if you cannot control yourself, permission to visit will be denied."

In the presence of the cadre, we turned to conversation about our children and my elderly mother. Our hour flew by, seeming like only minutes. With an aching heart, my parting advice to her was to never come back to see me again. With the sadness of her face indicating she understood why I would say such a difficult thing, we bade farewell. She and our neighbor then walked slowly away hand in hand, not turning back to look.

I could not sleep that night, thinking of my children and my wife, whose skinny appearance and greying hair indicated the hardship she had suffered since our separation. In the morning, I shared the food she brought with fellow prisoners who hadn't received any from their relatives. Later, three bedrooms were built in the visiting area far from our living quarters. The rooms were derisively referred to as "The House of Happiness" because only the wives of cooperative and "model" inmates, as defined by our captors, were permitted to spend a couple of nights there as a reward. If too many families arrived at the same time, chairs were arranged as makeshift beds in the visitor's parlor for the last to arrive.

The Thirteen Ghosts

In time, it became clear that the real reason the Communists had brought us to the north was to remove from the south those of us considered "dangerous elements," not to create better conditions for our reeducation, as they previously claimed. Those whose previous patriotism or present courage and determination caused them to be so labeled would be targeted to spend the rest of their lives deep in the jungles of the Thanh Phong secret zone in Thanh Hoa Province. We were told the lies that this was a rich and fertile area, which could be successfully farmed and in which cattle could be raised, that the government would provide us with seeds, equipment, machines, and tools, and that our families would resettle there with us for a better future. Thirteen were selected as pioneers to start the project, which was to be initiated as soon as possible. A former lieutenant general of the Republic of Vietnam Armed Forces was designated as the team leader, and the other twelve members selected were former officers of the engineer corps. They were dubbed "the thirteen ghosts" because we expected them to disappear and never be seen again. To entice the "volunteers," the project organizers showed them release orders complete with their names and the signature and seal of competent authority. Only the effective date of release was lacking. Furthermore, the team leader was given back his personal belongings, was allowed to wear them, and was permitted to be together with his wife and children shortly before departing for the secret zone. But, as an old saying proclaims, "man proposes, but God disposes," and, fortunately for the "volunteers," the secret zone relocation plan was canceled, probably, we reasoned, because of pressures from some outside source. The news that they, and we who were to follow, didn't have to spend the rest of our lives deep in the northern jungles was received with exhilaration. The "thirteen ghosts" returned to Ha Tay Camp, leaving the unfinished project behind them, and resumed the hard, humiliating routine as prisoners.

During the Tet holidays of February, 1982, rumors spread of the disbanding of Ha Tay Camp. Shortly thereafter, we were moved out of Ha Tay. On the move to our new destination we wore no handcuffs and carried our handbags on the buses with us. The camp cadres warmly wished us good luck, smiled, and waved farewell when the cars started rolling. Their newfound sympathy probably derived from the ironic fact that we, the inmates, had been helping our jailers by providing them medicines from the packages our families were sending us. From eyedrops to ointments and antibiotics, we gave them whatever they needed for their children. The result of their unexpected, warm wishes was that we left Ha Tay in an unprecedented, lighthearted mood, hoping that life at the next camp would be better.

Nam Ha Camp

Our convoy arrived at Nam Ha camp at dinnertime, and we were fed the same meager meal as at Ha Tay: rice, boiled vegetables, and salted water. The camp was located at the foothills of mountains that surrounded us and was constructed similarly to Ha Tay. The one major difference was a miniature mountain scene that was constructed in each zone's inner courtyard. From our upper-level room, I had a view of the distant mountains. On that first evening, the sight of thick, dreary clouds descending on the forbidding mountaintops filled my heart with a deep gloom.

The first week at Nam Ha was without work. The cadres reorganized our companies, merging our individual labor specialties with existing camp companies. The woodworking shop was very small in size, so we were given the additional work of cutting trees and obtaining palm branches for house construction. Several months later, another contingent of inmates arrived, including some who had left Thu Duc camp before I did. They told us that others had been sent back to camps in the south, but they didn't know how it was decided who would go.

I was now assigned to the fresh vegetable company. The cadre in charge of the company was a young officer who seemed sympathetic to our plight. In addition to caring for the primary vegetable beds of the camp, we were permitted to grow additional small plots for our own meals. The daily planting, watering, weeding, and destroying insects was well within our physical capabilities, except for the times we had to struggle to carry heavy loads of harvested vegetables back to the camp kitchen, or to gather and carry loads of animal excrement from stables about a kilometer away for use as fertilizer.

In general, the guards of Nam Ha camp had compassionate attitudes toward us, as most of them were older people who behaved with proper and quiet dignity. Now, after seven years of hard labor that had exhausted our strength, we felt consoled. With a canteen where food could be bought, and with provisions received from our families, our strength slowly returned. This new, easier policy toward us and the good news reported to us by some visiting families that foreign radio stations were publicizing the circumstances of our long imprisonment lifted our morale tremendously. I even began to have hope for a brighter future.

For the next five years, nothing changed, and each day was the same as the preceding one. We worked two shifts every weekday, but were allowed to rest on weekends. On those quiet days, we cooked for ourselves, walked, contemplated the fish in the small pool in the miniature mountain scene in our courtyard, or played the Asian version of chess.

I was now transferred from the green-vegetable company to the cooking company, where food was prepared for distribution to inmates in each room. As a newcomer to the company, I was assigned the job of cleaning the kitchen and taking fresh vegetables to each room, where the inmates now could cook them as they wanted. As small as this privilege might seem, it was important to us because the vegetables were no longer boiled for us as before. Thankfully, the cooking company could rest when we completed our chores, but we had to work every day, including Saturdays, Sundays, and holidays. Now and then, our tasks were difficult, as when we had to struggle with weakened bodies to carry one hundred–kilogram sacks of rice from supply trucks to the kitchen storage room.

On special occasions such as the National Holiday and Tet, our company was kept busy killing pigs, oxen, and water buffalo for rare treats for both the cadres and inmates. Thinking back to those times, I still become saddened by the recollection of one very old water buffalo that appeared to be actually shedding real tears as he was being led on feeble legs to the execution spot. It struck me that he must have known that death was awaiting him. After being smashed on the head by heavy hammer blows, he slowly fell to his knees. Up to that time, I had never eaten water buffalo meat, and I have not been able to do so from that experience until today.

Over the long and difficult twelve years of imprisonment, I suffered through extreme ranges of emotions and feelings. Sometimes, I was able to keep my spirits up and remain optimistic and hopeful. Other times, I sank into deep despair and depression. These swings of emotions became particularly deep and draining when some inmates began to be released. First, one at a time, then, in groups of ten, increasing numbers were being released. Slowly, those of us remaining began to have faith and hope that our turn also might come. Such prayerful hope was dashed when we got word that some of those released were picked up again and taken to Hoa Lo Prison in Hanoi for continued investigation and interrogation. In time, some of my former roommates were returned to our camp after suffering brutalities called "working sessions" in Hoa Lo, not fully comprehending what had happened to them and why.

The final and irrevocable release by death continued to come to many. Professor X. died of a stomach ulcer and inmate L. died of leukemia. General N. passed away from prostate cancer, Colonel Ph. Nh. H. from tuberculosis, and Colonel H. and General Q. from strokes. These were the only deaths that I witnessed, but there were many more which I did not see.

Unlike the Long Thanh and Thu Duc camps in the south, the two northern camps, Ha Tay and Nam Ha, were used to detain both political and criminal prisoners. One big difference in the northern camps where I was detained was that political prisoners were not subjected to physical punishment. Instead, sanctions were imposed that varied according to the degree of seriousness of the violation. These sanctions ranged from a warning before the company, to admonition before the entire camp, to suspension of the right to correspond with or receive gifts from the family for a period of time, to solitary confinement with legs shackled. A young man under thirty years of age, named B. B. D., was given such shackled confinement. For month after month, with one leg cuffed to his cement bed, he slept, ate, and relieved himself at the place of confinement. When finally released, he was like a shadow, unable to walk, only slowly limping with the aid of a crutch. When dealing with criminal inmates, on the other hand, cadres often kicked and punched them. Even "self-repentant" prisoners—those who had made sufficient progress in education and were employed as guards—were allowed to resort to whipping or clubbing to deal with unruly criminal inmates.

Foreign Observers

Around this time, delegations of foreign observers occasionally came to the camp on so-called fact-finding missions. Prior to their arrival, the camp authorities made sure that everything was arranged to appear meticulously proper and correct. Sewers were made operational and cleaned up. Toilet areas were made spotless and sanitary. Living quarters were put in perfect, orderly condition to present the impression that they were always maintained in that ideal condition. Companies that had to travel far to their work sites were hidden from sight while delegations were present. When the foreign teams arrived, their members came to see the products we made, but we were forbidden to talk with them. All visitor's questions were answered by the cadres. In order to give the impression that fewer inmates resided in our cramped, small sleeping spaces and that we all had adequate room, many of our blankets and mosquito nets were removed and hidden away. Sick inmates were removed from the infirmary and taken elsewhere before the visitors inspected the facility, and the library was temporarily filled with additional books and magazines that were conveniently being read by planted, attentive readers.

The largest delegation of foreign media representatives came to the camp in early February, 1988, to witness, film, and record a scheduled release of prisoners. Whether on purpose or not, the release was timed to coincide with the period immediately before the traditional Tet holidays. One month before the scheduled media delegation visit, a team of central administration cadres came to conduct "working" sessions with about one hundred inmates, dealing with a few each day. Those returning from these interview sessions were full of hope for being released in the near future. We all wished we would be chosen for interview, believing the interviews were an initial prerequisite for release.

Although at the time we were preparing for our Tet festivities, and found joy in such activity, the eagerness to be called for a "working" session with the cadre crowded out and overshadowed all our other thoughts. Most of the inmates of the cooking company were interviewed and subsequently put on the list of those selected to be freed. The company was then dissolved, and our cooking duties were passed on to the criminal prisoners.

When my time finally came, I was interviewed by a stern, elderly cadre. After checking my identity and background, he asked me what I would do after being released. I hoped my honest answer would be the correct one he was seeking, since I suspected his intention in asking it. When I finished, he stated that he would suggest my release, but the final decision was up to his superiors. He continued, saying that if I were released, I must continue my reeducation, abide by the laws of the nation, comply with all instructions from local authorities, and not participate in antirevolutionary organizations or activities. These admonitions, he explained, were the answers he expected to his question "What would you do after release?"

CHAPTER 5

Release

One week before Tet began, we were officially notified of our release and moved to a separate area away from the less lucky remaining inmates. Each of us was given dark gray pants and a white shirt, the uniform for the release ceremony. The celebration took place in a great hall outside the camp, attended by the camp chief, cadres from central administration, and the cadres of the camp, in addition to a delegation of more than twenty foreign media representatives. Inmate T. D. M. opened the ceremony with a thank-you speech written by him and carefully censored beforehand. His remarks were followed by a sermon from a central cadre assuring us that we would no longer be kept under surveillance and would be immediately reinstated as citizens when we returned to our localities. Regional authorities had been instructed to issue us an identification card and other services without delay. He finished by stating that he himself would pay personal visits to us to check on our treatment. After the ceremony, we were fingerprinted, and the release certificates were completed. As a final act of release, we were given some money for traveling from Saigon to our homes and the original copy of the release certificate.

We left the camp at noon on February 13, 1988—twelve years, seven months and twenty-seven days after I had reported for "one month of re-education"—and arrived at the Nam Dinh railway station at twilight. After an anxious, tense wait of ten hours, the southbound train finally arrived. One entire car was reserved for us and the two armed guards who escorted us to Saigon. We arrived in Saigon, fittingly, on February 17, the last day of the concluding lunar year and, symbolically, the end of my imprisonment and separation from my family. I bade farewell to my comrades and quickly boarded a cyclo for home.

En route through the city, many places previously so familiar to me were now greatly changed. Many were unrecognizable, some more beautiful, but most more rundown and dirty. The sun was setting low in the sky when I arrived at my home. My eldest daughter was busy sweeping the front yard and looked up to see who was trying to open the front gate. Overcome with emotion, she threw away her broom and loudly cried out, "Dad is home." Thus, my presence became known to the entire family, who were busily engaged in preparations to welcome the New Year.

As I entered the house and embraced my family, my heart overflowed with joy and happiness. The sight of surrounding, glittering-yellow apricot blossoms, the traditional symbol of the Vietnamese New Year, added to my pleasure, as the flowers also seemed to be welcoming me home on this auspicious occasion, holding out to the family long-repressed hopes for a better and brighter future.

After fully absorbing the happiness of the long-awaited reunion with my wife and children, I rushed to the house next door to see my mother. After years of longing and hoping to be reunited, she looked so very old. With tears in her eyes she warmly embraced me, asking why I looked so skinny. Hearing that expression of love, tears also flowed down my cheeks from the emotion and joy of seeing her still alive. Since the ritual of offering food to our departed ancestors had already finished, the entire family concentrated on sharing a joyous but all-too-fleeting celebration until midnight.

When the brief holiday was over, I had to return to reality and report my arrival home to the local public security office. As instructed, I submitted three copies of my biographical data to the ward cadre, then went to the office of city public security to accomplish other required formalities there. Finally, I reported to the district authorities to apply for my ID card. As promised by the officials from central administration in the north on the occasion of our release ceremony, I was now served without delay wherever I went. In fact, about one month after applying for my ID card, I received it.

CHAPTER 6

My Family's Years of Misery

During my thirteen years of hardship, my family suffered adversity, indignity, humiliation, fear, and deprivation of their own, being literally impoverished by the new regime. The ordeal began two days after I left home when four strangers arrived, looking for me. They introduced themselves to my wife as friends of mine who came from My Tho to see me. When she told them I was in reeducation, they left after first scrupulously inspecting our living room, probably to make sure I wasn't hiding there. My Tho is the capital of Dinh Tuong Province, where I had served seven years prior as the province chief. Surely, the strangers' story was false since I had no close and devoted friends in My Tho who would travel such a long way to see me, particularly immediately after the collapse of South Vietnam, a time when true friends more properly would have been taking care of themselves and their families. Moreover, true friends would not have been so discourteous as to abruptly leave without one parting word of courtesy. Had I been at home at the time, I'm sure I would have been arrested by those "friends" and taken back to Dinh Tuong for "people's justice." After April 30, 1975, there were numerous cases of reprisals perpetrated in the countryside by local Viet Cong cadres who sought revenge against people they labeled as antirevolutionaries who owed "blood debts" to the people. In many instances, reprisal took the form of summary execution following a brief, mock trial.

A short time after that, my wife was ordered to attend a five-day reeducation course along with all other teachers in her district. After completing the course, she was sent back to her original school to resume her teaching duties. One teacher, obviously affiliated with the revolution, was appointed principal. Empowered with full authority, that teacher completely changed all school activities, from administrative regulations to the way she dealt with and treated her colleagues. Teachers now had to work for former janitors who were elevated to supervisory positions. Female teachers had to wear the black *ao ba ba* instead of the graceful, traditional *ao dai.* All had to attend a night class each weekend and participate in monthly critique and self-criticism sessions.

During the first such session, the new principal singled out for criticism both Mrs. H. for having a brother, an army colonel who escaped abroad, and my wife for having "feudalism" deeply rooted in her background. The principal stated that the only way my wife could become an honest citizen was to scrub herself over and over again with soap, which she had to do until the resulting pain made her tears flow. As an honorable and devoted teacher for twenty years who was esteemed by her colleagues and respected by her students and their parents, my wife was deeply offended by such remarks, particularly coming from a former colleague who now, without honor and in harmony with the new Communist policy, berated the former regime and those who had honorably served it. As hard as my wife tried not to, she could not refrain from weeping openly. The entire audience was shocked and also offended by the venomous assertions that the new principal so disdainfully hurled at teachers whose only "offense" was that they were related to people considered "fake military" by the revolutionists.

From their very first day back in school, the teachers were disgusted with everything, material and ideological, derived from the new regime. The monthly salary was barely enough to support living for twenty days, even considering the minimal amounts of food available for purchase and the many other restrictions imposed on the population. Because of the shortage of cash to pay the teachers during some months, they were instead given some fabric as payment. They then had to sell the fabric at very low prices, which meant less money was available to buy rice and other necessary commodities. Because they were now the sole family wage earners and unable to make ends meet, any meager savings they had were soon spent to keep families alive and well. After exhausting all resources, many teachers asked to be allowed to resign, hoping to be able to find a better job. Their requests were always turned down because of the countrywide shortage of teachers,

The only way to survive was to get extra jobs after school hours, such as pedaling passenger cyclos or commodity-delivery tricycles, selling small items in the streets or at the market, and engaging in construction jobs. My wife's nighttime job was as a seamstress. After working day and night, year after year, because it was necessary to support the family, and additionally ordered by regional authorities to conduct reading classes to illiterates in their homes, my wife saw her health steadily decline. One night, as she pedaled home from a teaching class, she collapsed from exhaustion. After that, she was thankfully exempted from such extra required duties.

My children, each in their turn, returned to school, but they were not permitted to advance beyond high school because of their parents' collaboration with the old regime, called the "fake" military, the "imposter" military. Not having enough of what were considered acceptable "political grades" to be admitted to higher education, all my children had to get menial jobs requiring them to work hard from dawn to dusk. They peddled books and newspapers on the streets and also made clothing as my wife did. Their combined, meager earnings did not provide enough for them to quell their hunger or dress decently. To provide minimal nourishment, their rice had to be mixed with low quality cereals. South Vietnam had never been short of rice for its people, but now the people had to eat rice supplemented with manioc, potatoes, and *bo bo*. Every now and then, small amounts of meat and fish were sold at a cooperative station at prices lower than those at the market. However, people had to get a place in line before dawn to wait for the service to start. This was the way of life for families of the "fake" persons. Such a miserable life imposed by the Communists caused depression and despair of any improvement. The difficult situation was made worse by the increasing proliferation of thefts and robberies that now occurred. At night, robbers would cut gate chains and take pried-loose glass windows and ornamental plants in antique, colored, glazed pots, plus all other available items.

During an epidemic of conjunctivitis, no medicine was available to treat the disease, so all family members treated themselves with salt water. Normally a minor disease that quickly healed with proper medicine, the untreated, contagious conjunctivitis lingered on for more than a month.

One night, about five months after the Communist takeover, a group of armed cadres came to our house and ordered everyone to gather in the living room. A house requisition was read, which put my wife and children in a panic, huddling together and lamenting. Then a young man from the group whispered to my wife, "It is only for exchanging money." Only then was she reassured enough to calm our distraught children. The house was then temporarily used as a place for nearby residents to come and change old money for new currency. At another time, our house was requisitioned and used as a station for casting ballots.

When I finally returned home, I understood the many hardships my wife and children suffered. My wife had had to sell her engagement ring, an irreplaceable keepsake, to help her prepare for her trip to visit me at Ha Tay Camp. Following their mother's example, my children sold the gifts I had rewarded them with upon their previous graduations. They used the money to help buy and send food packages to me and to contribute to the family's many other needs. Upon learning this, my heart swelled with pride for the sacrifices they made supporting me and patiently awaiting my return.

CHAPTER 7

The Final Years

During this protracted time after my release, we experienced many mixed emotions as well as hopes and prayers for improving our lives. One rare and most uplifting and encouraging occurrence was hearing news from the Voice of America and the British Broadcasting Corporation radio stations of the establishment of a program for the resettlement of reeducated people in the United States. A short time thereafter, brief details were published in Ho Chi Minh City daily newspapers that included a list of those already granted letters of introduction by the U.S. government. Remaining names were to be published weekly. We eagerly rushed to get and complete the papers required to obtain exit visas under the Humanitarian Operation, or HO, then anxiously waited.

Although the first contingent of departees left Vietnam in early 1990, it was early August, 1993, before our turn came. Following the advice of my predecessors, I signed a contract with the Ho Chi Minh City Emigration Service Center to make sure that all in my family would receive exit passports and would have their names entered on the departure lists required to be transmitted to the Orderly Departure Program Office, where applicants would be summoned for interview. I had to also pay for the services of another agency that was in charge of booking departure flights and registering permitted baggage. Advised by an employee of the agency that a tip of three hundred thousand Vietnamese *dong* (the equivalent of about thirty U.S. dollars) would ensure untroubled passage of my luggage through final inspection, I paid him that amount.

Later, at Tan Son Nhut Airport, the luggage did, in fact, pass the inspector without inspection. Before my turn came, I witnessed others who had their fully packed suitcases thoroughly emptied and searched, requiring not-so-patient repacking amid the crowded, busy terminal surroundings. It was my good fortune to have been in previous contact with relatives abroad who provided me with the required financial support, permitting me to pay the various out-processing expenses, which totaled about 150 U.S. dollars.

As all on earth is controlled by destiny, two and a half years before my departure, in early February, 1991, my mother had passed away at the age of ninety-five, sparing her the sorrow of the approaching separation from her only son. My deep sadness was without regret, though, because I was able to be there at the mourning ceremony, offering veneration, respect, and appreciation to a dear mother, and then subsequently was able to take care of her tomb. The tears I shed at her earthly parting also reinforced my courage to seek freedom abroad from the sadness of our once-happy land.

On the memorable day of our departure, we were filled with strong and mixed feelings. Close relatives, friends, and students and their parents came to Tan Son Nhut Airport to see us off. There were many hugs and tears from students wishing my wife a safe journey with good health while traveling. Everybody waved farewell as we departed the waiting area of the terminal, and all hearts were filled with deep emotion. After a short flight, we arrived in Thailand, where we had to stay for sixteen days before we could resume our journey to the United States. After eighteen years of separation, I couldn't wait to be reunited with my cousin-sponsor, Mrs. H. T. T., and her sister.

They and some other friends came to meet us on our arrival, exchanging great feelings of joy and thanksgiving. During those first days in our new country of freedom, my siblings and relatives extended their full support to us with warm and meticulous care, and mere words could never adequately express our gratitude. Soon, joyous calls from friends of yesteryear jammed my phone all day long. The most moving event was when I heard the familiar voice of Col. Edward P. Metzner, a U.S. advisor who worked side by side with me in Dinh Tuong Province, sharing the same ideology in the fight to preserve and protect freedom for South Vietnam. He had persevered in his efforts to search for me after April 30, 1975, and learning of his patience in doing so brought me immense joy as we conversed on the phone for a very long time, during which many memories of our friendship were recalled. He consoled me and encouraged me to recount what happened to me and my family after the black April of 1975, which I have done on the preceding pages.

A short time after my arrival in the United States, I volunteered to serve with the Multi Service Center (MSC) in Kirkland, Washington, a nonprofit organization. At present, I still continue to work for MSC's food bank. I hope that such an expression of good will on my part has engendered, and will continue to engender, mutual respect and empathy among the MSC staff members and my many volunteer colleagues. My wife is busy as the family homemaker, and my children have been happily resuming their studies. The whole family keeps strong faith for a bright future in this land of hope.

PART II

Col. Huynh Van Chinh's Story

CHAPTER 8

Advisory Days

The VC base area in Cang Long District, Vinh Binh Province, had been a thorn in the government's side, dating back to the days of the Viet Minh and the French. Nothing had changed when I arrived in Vinh Binh on my third tour in 1970. The IV Corps' plan to speed the pacification of the base area was centered around an ambitious effort to rebuild Route 6A, which pierced its center. Work on the road had stopped a year before my arrival. The reasons were a spate of VC sabotage, attacks on work crews, and the inability of the lightly armed province militia to protect the widely spread engineer units assigned to the repair task. As a result, the project had been abandoned instead of postponed when the last rainy season had come.

With the help of John Vann, deputy senior advisor at IV Corps, I pressured the corps to proceed again with construction of the road. In addition to sending back the engineer units, the corps assigned a regiment from the 9th Division to shield the engineers by conducting aggressive offensive operations. The regiment's command post was to be located in the heart of the base area.

On one of my periodic jeep trips to check on construction progress of the road and to spur it along if it was lagging, I noticed that the regiment's command post was completed and in operation. On the return trip, I stopped to introduce myself and to inquire about their plans. To my surprise and pleasure, the regimental commander turned out to be an old friend from my first tour of duty with the 7th Vietnamese Infantry Division in My Tho in 1964. Col. Huynh Van Chinh had then been Captain Chinh, chief of the division's Tactical Operations Center six years earlier when I was the division psychological warfare and pacification advisor.

Although we resumed our friendship, Chinh and I worked together only periodically because my counterpart was the Vinh Binh province chief and Chinh had his own advisor. Two years later, in 1972, destiny brought us together again for one last time on my fourth and final tour. This time, our official relationship would be most active and close. Chinh was the province chief of Kien Giang Province, and I was assigned as his advisor.

Those days working together in both civil government and military operations were very successful and productive, partially because of our lengthy mutual respect and trust. The main reason for our success, however, had nothing to do with the merit and value of my advice. It was solely the result of Chinh's competent and forceful personal-example style of leading his administrative staff and military commanders. While the solid and continuous progress that was shaped in the military and pacification fields brought great professional and ethical gratification to me, the personal highlight of my tour in Kien Giang was of an unofficial nature. Chinh introduced me to a lovely lady who soon thereafter became my wife. It happened this way.

After the so-called cease-fire agreement was signed in Paris in early 1973, I received advanced notice of plans to begin phasedown and closeout of the province advisory team. As part of the overall total pullout of U.S. armed forces, we were all to be out of the country by March 31 that year. After a long day working on the initial phase of the plan, which world remove all the district teams, I was tired and depressed. It was already dark when I drove my jeep to my quarters.

As I passed the only tennis court in the province, Colonel Chinh waved and called for me to stop. He told me to go and change and come back quickly to play, because he had a surprise for me. Over his shoulder I glimpsed his surprise: a pretty lady in a tasteful tennis dress was sitting and watching the foursome on the court. After quickly gulping down some dinner, I jogged back to the courts.

Chinh introduced me to Madame Pham and said his surprise was that I was to play a set against her. While the match in progress concluded, I leaned across Chinh to make polite conversation with Madame Pham. When I asked where she was from, she returned a beautiful smile and shook her head to show she spoke no English. Using Vietnamese as best I could, I found out that she was a teacher in the French high school system in Saigon and that she and Chinh had been schoolmates long ago. Suddenly the match in progress finished, and Chinh waved us onto the court.

Starting with the first ball she powered past me, Chinh's real surprise and my humiliation on the court began. The pretty lady was as commanding on the court as she was off it. She whistled her serves and volleys past me, making me run back and forth while desperately trying to reach her accurately placed strokes. When she decided to finish my struggles, she fired the ball where I had no chance of reaching it. Chinh and the others watching were having a wonderful time enjoying my agony until I held up my hand and my racket, walked to the net, and pleaded that I'd had enough.

As Madame Pham continued to play another opponent, I sat down heavily beside Chinh, and he explained the pleasant joke. Madame Pham was the Vietnamese national women's tennis champion, and he had invited her to the province capital to play exhibition matches. She was flying back to Saigon in the morning. Not knowing when I would see her again, I boldly asked her if she would have dinner with me the next time I visited Saigon. Her smile gave the answer before she said yes and told me how to get a message to her. When I was later chosen at the last minute to remain in Saigon, assigned to the Defense Attaché Office of the U.S. Embassy, I courted and married her.

When the order came to commence the final phase of withdrawal of U.S. military from Kien Giang and the date was set for my own departure, Chinh gave a farewell dinner for me. At the end of the party, Chinh and I retired to his house as previously planned. I wanted us to be alone when we discussed the last of my monthly assessment and recommendation letters to him. The letter was longer than previous ones because so many of our plans would be left undone, and I was charged with sadness and emotion when I wrote it.

This letter and our talk regarding it will be the last of our many discussions about the war, your people, and the future. I thought about what the future holds for Vietnam as I traveled around during Tet, and watched with a warm heart the many happy and hopeful faces of all the beautiful children. That experience brought back clearly to my mind what I heard often in the past from many Vietnamese people including farmers, soldiers, and government officials. They all said, in essence, "We are making our sacrifices today to ensure a peace with freedom and happiness for our children in the future." In so very many families only the children remain, waiting for that world of peace and happiness that their parents sacrificed to obtain for them. The cost paid by the good and brave Vietnamese people in suffering, tragedy, and death is enormous.

The sacrifice and cost paid by my country is also great. More than fifty thousand Americans died to attain a future that will include peace with freedom for your beautiful land. As a soldier who has spent almost one-fifth of my life and nearly half of my army service in Vietnam as your comrade-in-arms, I can say with emphatic sincerity that my government has pursued that ultimate goal with honor and integrity. You will recall that when I first returned to Kien Giang, I said that because I know you, I also know you are an outstanding, competent leader who really didn't need an advisor.

With that in mind, I write this letter to you not as your advisor but as the personal friend, trusted ally, and comrade-in-arms, which I consider myself fortunate to have been since we first met nine years ago in 1964.

Throughout the letter, I recalled needs we had often discussed at length: for the government to continue improving the lives of the people if the people were to support the government; for developing leadership and integrity in the lower ranks of the province forces; for good civil administration; and for keeping corruption from burdening those on the lowest rungs of the socio-economic ladder. In closing, I reemphasized that the side that got the support of the people ultimately would win. Although, when he finished reading, Chinh characteristically simply stood and thanked me for everything, I was confident that he would continue pursuing these critical objectives. We shook hands and said good night, pretending that my departure was merely one of many other such previous nightly farewells.

In the morning, Chinh was waiting at the airfield to see me off. One of the advisory team's Vietnamese civilian employees produced a bottle of red wine for a final toast. When the toast was finished and farewells were said, I turned toward Chinh, snapped him a final salute, and jumped aboard the helicopter. It was February 26, 1973. It would be another twenty-three years before we found each other again, thirteen of which Chinh spent in North Vietnamese prisons.

CHAPTER 9

Background

I am not a writer, so my words and composition are not smooth and clear, and may not satisfy the reader. I take up my pen not to impress you, but, rather, for the honor of the Army of the Republic of Vietnam. During the war against the Communists, many reporters among the nationalists and our allies unfairly belittled the military spirit of the South Vietnamese armed forces, and consequently we suffered the result of April 30, 1975, when the south fell into the hands of the Communists.

I speak on behalf of the spirit of the South Vietnamese army. Some may say that because I was an officer, I am only protecting the reputation of my forces. Such a judgment is, I think, unfair, for as I write about what happened, anyone can read and judge for themselves, thus I cannot speak on the army's account without offering concrete evidence. With twenty-one years' service as a soldier and thirteen more years as a prisoner of the Communists, I am now more than sixty years old. What accolade or benefit could I gain by promoting myself? I do, however, write for my personal honor as an officer, as well as for the honor of the entire Army of the Republic of Vietnam.

I was born on July 11, 1934, in the village of Tan An in Cang Long District, Tra Vinh Province, to a family of middle-class farmers. As a child I attended the village preparatory and elementary schools. In 1942, during the Second World War, I passed the exam to advance to the next level and went to the district school for two years. But the war spread—Japan toppled the French administration, then later surrendered to the Allies in 1945. In early 1946 the French returned and took control of my village, but by the end of the year they had to abandon it to the Viet Minh because it was too remote to supply.

At that time I was attending the district school. Hearing about the French withdrawal from my village, I quickly returned home to see my parents.

However, I was held by the Viet Minh because my second-oldest brother was a sergeant in the French colonial army and my sister lived in Saigon. The Viet Minh watched us and restricted our movement. When our village was later raided by the French, involving intense artillery fire, my family was caught in the middle, because both the French and the Viet Minh considered us the enemy. My only recourse was to escape to the French zone during the violence of the battle. I tried to evade the Viet Minh by night, but was seen and pursued to the city of Tra Vinh, where I arrived safely at 2 o'clock the next morning. My brother in the French army sponsored me, so the police did not arrest me as a suspected Viet Minh supporter. With help from my brother and sister, I completed the fifth level of the province school in 1949. The following year I went to Saigon, where I earned a diploma in 1953.

On March 26, 1954, I passed the entrance examination and was accepted into the Reserve Officers Training Academy in Thu Duc. I was there when the Geneva Accords were signed on July 20, 1954, dividing the country into two political zones. In October of that year I graduated with the rank of second lieutenant. Two weeks after graduation, I was assigned to Bac Lieu Sector in the Mekong Delta.

From 1954 to 1972 I served in the Army of the Republic of Vietnam (ARVN) as a platoon leader, company commander, battalion commander, then regimental commander in the 9th Infantry Division. From January, 1972, to October, 1974, I was the province chief in Kien Giang. It was during this latter period that I met Col. Edward Metzner, who was my advisor.

CHAPTER 10

The Beginning of the End

In December, 1974, I was assigned as assistant division commander for operations of the 7th Infantry Division. The 7th was under the command of Brig. Gen. Tran Van Hai, who was also chief of staff for the technical units stationed at the former U.S. base at Dong Tam in Dinh Tuong Province, located west of the province capital of My Tho.

Division combat units included the 11th Regiment, stationed in the Hau My area deep in the Viet Cong secret zone of Dong Thap, north of National Route 4 (NR4); the 10th Regiment, in the western part of Dinh Tuong by My Thuan Ferry, which crossed the Tien Giang River to Vinh Long Province; and the 12th Regiment, stationed in the Cai Lay central province area. The 10th and 12th Regiments were division mobile forces. Reserves included the 6th Armored Squadron, three 105–mm field artillery battalions, and one 155–mm field artillery battalion. The 7th Division was responsible for security in the provinces of Dinh Tuong, Kien Hoa, Go Cong, and Kien Phong. Within our tactical area of responsibility (TAOR) the most vital mission was the security of National Route 4, which ran the length of Dinh Tuong Province from My Thuan Ferry in the southwest to the northeast border with Long An Province. This most important road was the main supply artery between the rice-producing provinces of the Mekong Delta and Saigon.

When I assumed my duties with the 7th Infantry Division in 1974, security in the TAOR was stable. There were no major enemy confrontations, only occasional incidents of local Viet Cong forces' harassing isolated guard posts. Our division conducted regular clearing operations throughout the TAOR, but enemy main force units evaded contact by retreating into the Dong Thap secret zone, also known as the Plain of Reeds.

Meanwhile, the enemy situation in Military Region I (MR I) was becoming active. By January, 1975, things in MR III, which bordered our own MR IV to the north, were also becoming tense. The enemy employed division units brought in from the north to attack MR III's 5th Division. Still, at this time there were no serious losses. As for the area under the command of the 7th, enemy activity remained limited to scattered incidents of harassment in remote locations.

The Unfolding of Events

In early February, 1975, the Viet Cong stepped up activity in MR III, including simultaneous attacks against the province and district capitals of Phuoc Long Province near the Cambodian border, about 125 kilometers north of Saigon. This was the start of the enemy's final major campaign. After many days, they occupied all of Phuoc Long, inflicting heavy casualties on our forces, who fought until they were overrun, with all defenders killed, wounded, or captured. Phuoc Long was an isolated province, and all supply, communication, and reinforcement routes into it had been cut, so these functions had to be accomplished by air. The ARVN MR III command had plans for reinforcement and counterattack, but our soldiers could not be sent in by air because of enemy shelling of airfields. The advance of North Vietnamese Army (NVA) tanks and coordinated ground action by Viet Cong divisions further frustrated relief plans. In the end, Saigon had no recourse but to abandon Phuoc Long to the enemy.

Although I was a colonel at the level of a combat division, I rarely considered or fully understood the political situation being pondered at the higher levels; rather, my mission and focus was local security. During my spare time I read the newspapers, but they were sketchy and inaccurate, and only the higher echelons were briefed on the whole picture. In retrospect, I believe this was one of the shortcomings of my government. During a previous assignment I had had some involvement in political matters, so I understood the Paris Accords of 1973, including the arguments and positions of the Hanoi and Saigon governments, and the clause that stipulated U.S. retaliatory strikes if the Communists violated the agreement. Thus I was certain that the capture of Phuoc Long was a test of America's reaction.

When the United States failed to respond, the Viet Cong continued to violate the peace accords by attacking in turn the upper provinces of MR I with forces five times stronger than those used against Phuoc Long. In

MR II the Viet Cong exerted simultaneous pressure on the provinces bordering Laos. During this time, security concerns in the 7th Division's TAOR were still restricted to isolated incidents of harassment, and there were no major battles.

At the end of February, Tra On District in Vinh Long was subjected to pressure from the Viet Cong's D3 Regiment, which surrounded outposts and forced their defenders to fall back toward the district capital. Tra On District lay next to the Hau Giang River, about 20 kilometers south of NR4. By early March, Viet Cong main force units captured the posts on the interprovincial road between Vinh Long Province and Cang Long District, Vinh Binh Province. Meanwhile, the section of NR4 from Cai Lay to Cai Be in Dinh Tuong Province was obstructed by Viet Cong sabotage and mines every night.

General Hai, the division commander, realized the situation was becoming serious, so he called me back from mobile operations to assist him with mobilization and command. I organized actions to reduce pressure on NR4, which now was beginning to feel constant pressure from the Viet Cong's 8th Upper Delta Division.

At every morning briefing, I now paid attention to the situation in MR I and MR II. Basing my assessment on intelligence supplied by the general staff and indicated on the map, I became quite pessimistic, for it seemed that every twenty-four hours we lost one province, while resistance seemed to weaken in another. Every morning, the red pins showing enemy units on the map were moved farther south.

Despite this, we maintained overall security throughout our zone, and I remained confident we could continue to do so. The 7th Division maintained operations along NR4 and in the provinces under our responsibility, and continued to seek out the enemy, although there were no major confrontations.

By early April, 1975, Viet Cong main force units had begun large-scale attacks on outposts along the border between Vinh Binh and Vinh Long Provinces, with the intention of cutting the major communications route to Saigon. NR4 was damaged in many places by the enemy's actions. At the same time, regional force outposts fell in the Dong Thap region (the Plain of Reeds) in Kien Phong Province.

Our MR I forces completed withdrawal to MR II and gradually slipped remaining units farther south to Phan Rang, capital of Ninh Thuan Province. There, a defense was organized against the advancing wave of the North Vietnamese Army.

During this period—I don't recall exactly when—I learned that military and civilian administrative leaders of MR I, and many from MR II as well, were being held by the national government on charges of abandoning their positions and fleeing south without putting up a serious resistance. These officials were initially kept under guard at Cong Hoa Military Hospital in Saigon, and were later transferred to the headquarters of the general staff to await final disposition of their cases. I phoned a friend who was one of the commanders from MR I now in Saigon, to ask how he was doing. He recommended that I come to Saigon to talk with him directly because it was not a good idea to discuss those matters over the telephone. I did not feel that I could leave my place of duty at this time because the situation in the 7th Division's area was becoming unstable.

Our situation continued to remain quiet during the day, except that some remote and isolated outposts exposed to increasing enemy pressure had to be abandoned. On the last Saturday of April, the Long An province headquarters, located northeast of our headquarters, reported a large number of Viet Cong moving toward the Long An airfield from the vicinity of the Thay Cai canal bordering the Plain of Reeds. At the same time, a report from one of the 7th Division's artillery units attached to Long An and stationed at the airfield confirmed the enemy's movement.

In the first light of dawn, the artillery unit could clearly make out waves of Viet Cong advancing toward the airfield, and they requested specific orders. General Hai and I were present in the Tactical Operations Center (TOC) and ordered direct artillery fire on the enemy units. The resulting heavy casualties caused the enemy to break off their attack and disperse into nearby villages, deploying their main defensive line on the edge of a village belonging to Khanh Hau on NR4, about ten kilometers from Long An.

Meanwhile, Long An sector garrison headquarters now reported the presence of an NVA division that, according to our information, had to be the 9th Work Group (the 9th Division), also coming from Dong Thap on the border of Long An. The 9th had crossed the Vam Co River and attacked Thu Thua District near the city of Long An, and was now advancing toward NR4 between the bridges at Cau Voi and Cau Van, so as to cut all traffic flowing between Long An and Saigon. Since Long An was closer to the 7th Division's TAOR than to its parent MR III headquarters, we had prior permission to coordinate and provide necessary support to that province.

Concerned about the strong enemy action so close to the 7th Division's TAOR, General Hai ordered an attack against the enemy at Khanh Hau that day. The effort involved our 12th Regiment and 6th Armored Squadron, supported by artillery and air cover. It was a difficult operation, since one regiment of Work Force 9 had been assigned to block relief efforts to Long An, as well as cut off any traffic from Saigon to the Delta.

Knowing for certain we were facing the NVA, we went all out to attack our objective. The North Vietnamese soldiers were regulars who had modern weapons and were fully equipped by the Russians and Chinese. Nonetheless, they were mostly inexperienced youths with little battle experience, unfamiliar with the terrain and quite frightened.

After many hours of fighting, the 7th seized its objective around 3 o'clock that afternoon and regained control of the village. Our after-action assessment revealed that we had destroyed an enemy regiment, captured many soldiers, often below the age of 18, and taken weapons and ammunition, along with electronic gear such as Chinese radios, telephones, and thousands of meters of wire. This confirmed that the enemy unit was a major one composed of NVA regulars, not Viet Cong, because such units always established communications among company, battalion, and regiment headquarters by telephone landlines, rather than by less secure radio communication. While the 7th was engaged in mopping up and reestablishing security on NR4 in and around Khanh Hau and to the south, the NVA remained in control of the highway between the Cau Voi and Cau Van bridges just a few kilometers to our north.

In Dinh Tuong Province now, every night was the same. About 3 o'clock each morning, Cai Be and Cai Lay Districts would inform headquarters that the Viet Cong had destroyed long stretches of NR4 with mines. Disregarding the danger, General Hai and I downed our coffee and headed by open jeep to Cai Lay. We went there in order to personally supervise and urge aggressive counteractions by Colonel Son, the assistant area commander, Col. Truong Ky, the engineer in charge of repairing NR4, and Lieutenant Colonel Pham, the commander of the 6th Armored Squadron. Together, we then rushed to the place the Viet Cong had destroyed, accompanied by vehicles loaded with rocks and interlaced iron matting to fix the road so that early morning food convoys could proceed to Saigon. Once we barely escaped injury on such a repair mission when time-delay fused mines exploded only fifteen meters away from us.

The stretch of road from Cau Voi to Cau Van in Long An Province was being held at all cost by the Communists' 9th Work Force. The 7th Infantry could have uprooted them in a day at most, but that area remained under control of MR III, and, at this time, the distinguished commanders of MR

III were busy packing their belongings to flee the country with their families, so they had no time to worry about freeing a stretch of highway or giving permission to MR IV to do it. Thus unimpeded, the enemy controlled the road, and any four-wheeled or two-wheeled vehicles that passed were fired on. This was obviously done to isolate units in the delta and to prevent any of our high-ranking government officials from disguising themselves as civilians and escaping to the Mekong Delta.

Around April 28, the Viet Cong's local 8th Division lay six kilometers north of NR4 in Dinh Tuong and was coordinating with Viet Cong main force regiments to attack the highway. They could not achieve their objective, however, because the 10th and 12th Regiments and the 6th Armored Squadron were deployed there to meet them.

In Vinh Binh Province to the south, Viet Cong local units succeeded in occupying some remote outposts. They also seized control of the road between Vinh Binh and Vinh Long, but after several hours were driven back deep into the jungle. A local Viet Cong regiment also temporarily seized the Vinh Long Province NR4 area between Binh Minh and Ba Cang, intending to cut traffic from Can Tho City to the north. However, they were quickly driven off by the 16th Regiment of the ARVN 9th Division, and suffered heavy casualties.

On the morning of April 29, all of MR IV, and in particular the 7th Division's TAOR, remained firmly under friendly control. Military and civil officials went to work as usual, civilians went about their daily business as though nothing was going on, and daytime traffic on NR4 continued flowing freely to Saigon, bypassing the Cau Voi and Cau Van bridge blockades via a detour through Go Cong Province.

Around noon, a civilian bus full of students struck a landmine near Cai Lay. General Hai and I immediately went out there to assess the situation. A horrible scene greeted us. Innocent students lay dead and wounded, scattered about the highway. I called for the 9th Medical Battalion to send out ambulances to transport the wounded to the 3rd Field Hospital in My Tho. General Hai and I then continued on to Cai Lay and ordered the district chief to step up night security activity by the road outposts, and to commit additional local units to the task.

As night came, our headquarters fell silent, everyone now beginning to contemplate tomorrow and his own fate. General Hai conferred with the staff to evaluate the situation, after which I napped in the TOC in order to be ready in case of further emergencies. Despite being very busy with normal military duties, plus planning further countermeasures and spoiling actions, I still found some time to follow developing news on the radio. I knew that President Thieu had resigned and that Mr. Tran Van Huong had taken his place, then also resigned, passing the presidency on to Gen. Duong Van Minh. I saw clearly what was happening in Saigon and to the north, yet still felt that we could continue to hold the Mekong Delta since the Communists had not been able to take and hold any important points. At this time, I felt it was odd that General Hai did not discuss the overall situation with me. After meeting privately with visiting generals and ranking civilians, he would just continue his routine of smoking cigarettes and pacing the hallway with his hands behind his back, sometimes breaking into a strange, sad smile.

Early the next morning, the 7th Division received the order from MR IV to group our regiments and armored squadron and coordinate with the 9th Infantry Division, now in My Tho, to attack and regain control of the part of NR4 that had been cut off by the Viet Cong since April 21. As we prepared to move out and execute the order, the commander of MR IV, General Nam, canceled it and sent us back to await further instructions. General Hai and I returned perplexed to Dong Tam headquarters with the rest of the operations staff.

At about 10 o'clock, MR IV ordered the 7th Division to lay down our arms and turn over command to the Communists, in accordance with President Duong Van Minh's proclamation. After receiving a phone call from his wife, General Hai entered his office and shut the door behind him.

When President Minh's message of surrender to the Viet Cong reached the units supporting division headquarters, the men were in shock. Soldiers abandoned their weapons and rushed with their wives and children out the front gate. Around 2 o'clock in the afternoon, General Hai circled the compound in his jeep to see what was happening. In anger, he leaped from his vehicle and plunged into the crowd of fleeing soldiers, kicking, punching, and shouting in vain at them to return to their posts.

Around 3 o'clock that afternoon, as General Hai and I were waiting in the TOC for further orders from General Nam, a member of the Viet Cong local 8th Division came in over our radio net requesting to speak with the commander of F7 (the 7th Division). General Hai had me answer. I took the radio.

"This is the commander speaking. Go ahead."

"Did you hear your president's order to surrender?" inquired the voice on the other end. "We ask you to raise a white flag for the revolution to take over."

"We have not yet received such an order on our phone," I responded, "and we cannot carry out any order from you coming over the radio."

The voice on the other end urged us to lay down our arms and come out to the road crossing to greet them, there officially handing over command of our units to them under a white flag.

General Hai had me make the arrangements. I answered the other side by declaring that we would not fly a white flag since we had not surrendered, but they insisted that we turn over command to them. While this discussion was going back and forth, the enemy was advancing toward NR4. I ordered all our armored personnel carriers stationed along the highway to fire on them to stop them. The Viet Cong retreated to nearby villages to wait. Their commander asked us to cease firing on their soldiers, to which I replied, "We have not yet concluded our discussions. Your soldiers cannot move forward on the road. We do not surrender, and we do not raise a white flag." The Viet Cong commander reported to his superiors that we would not fly a white flag, and this was subsequently accepted. By nightfall, both sides agreed that we would remain in place until the next morning, May 1. At that time our representatives would meet on NR4, then proceed to our headquarters, where we would turn over command.

That night, I asked the division's air force liaison officer if the two L19 observation airplanes had fuel. He replied that they could reach the U.S. 7th Fleet, but added that he could not leave his family behind. Upon reflection, I knew I could not leave mine either. Although most telephone lines from the TOC were not operational, we were still in communication with our units by radio. I contacted the navy patrol boat commander who patrolled the nearby My Tho River up to Vinh Long. He offered to take me to the 7th Fleet, but he did not think he would have enough time to stop in Vinh Long and get my family. I declined the offer, then called my wife, telling her not to take the children anywhere, but to wait at home by the telephone.

I found a bottle of Hennessy cognac along with some pork cold cuts. Pouring a glass, I invited the officers present with me to drink, toasting our uncertain fate. Around midnight we fell asleep right where we sat.

When I awoke abruptly the next morning, the base was all but deserted. I roused the others, and we prepared to go our separate ways. We sadly shook hands for the last time before heading home to our families to seek a means of escape. As I stepped outside, I felt depressed and pitied the soldiers under my authority rushing out the gate, discarding their uniforms, carrying their children, and leading their wives outside the compound.

At division headquarters, I learned that General Hai had taken his own life. It seems that after our radio conversation with the Viet Cong the night before, he had retired to his quarters, where, shutting the door behind him, he took a heavy dose of sleeping pills. The other staff and command officers and I felt we were not in a position now to hand over command to the Communists.

I changed into civilian clothes and filled a small briefcase with about 120,000 piastres (about 250 U.S. dollars) and joined the soldiers fleeing helter-skelter on the road. It was the same road our division had traveled many times during military operations. I cannot describe the scene—motorcycles, cars, and especially the hordes of people fleeing toward My Tho, most of them soldiers from our division.

Along the way, we encountered a checkpoint manned by five or six male and female armed guerrillas. As others were having their papers checked, I slipped past and continued on. At another checkpoint outside of My Tho, I showed the guards a civilian ID. They inspected my briefcase and asked where all the money was from. I told them I was the boss of a brickworks and was in the process of collecting payments when I got caught in the course of events. They told me to move on, which I did without hesitation.

Meanwhile, Communist cadres using loudspeakers advised everyone to remain calm and not panic. Here and there, I saw a few young people making propaganda. They said, "The country is at peace! Brother soldiers of the former rebel authorities, return to your families and resume your occupations! The Provisional Revolutionary Government shall not take revenge! Return home and await the orders of the revolution!"

I hurried to find a Lambretta, a type of minibus powered by a motor scooter, to take me to NR4 on the outskirts of My Tho City. Once there, I waited for a bus or a lift from one of the small rented cars heading west from Saigon. You cannot imagine the scene. The traffic was heavy, and all the cars were going away from Saigon toward the delta, while not one was going in the opposite direction. All vehicles large and small were packed, some with passengers riding on the roofs and hanging from the sides. The scene was awful, chaotic! I waited from 8 o'clock until noon before a small car stopped for me. As I looked on both sides of the road, I could not contain my emotions, and my eyes teared as I saw armored personnel carriers abandoned with discarded uniforms and weapons flung beside them.

We reached My Thuan Ferry to Vinh Long at 2 o'clock, but cars were backed up from the loading dock for several kilometers. I walked some three or four kilometers to the ferry. The scene was more chaotic. The newly arrived Viet Cong had no idea how to properly operate a ferryboat, and the dockworkers and pilots had already fled. I made my way through the crowd and waited aboard the ferry until it finally, haltingly took me to the north shore at Vinh Long, where I then hopped on a Lambretta and went home.

It was sunset when I arrived, and my wife and children were elated to see me. My wife was the quiet kind, but the look on her face now clearly revealed her concern. The children were openly fearful and anxious. I kissed them, then went upstairs without bothering to clean up and fell on the bed exhausted, wondering what was to become of us. The country was now lost, and families were widely dispersed. The chaos affected even our dog, whom the children loved so. When it heard my voice, it had bolted across the road and was run over by a Viet Cong military truck. One additional reason for the children to weep.

After I had a little food and rest, some visitors arrived. A few friends tried to convince us that things would be all right and that the Communists would not try to exact revenge against anyone. I disagreed, but kept my thoughts to myself. Other neighbors urged us to get out as quickly as possible. My concern was that I would be found out, immediately arrested, and taken from the family. Everything, it seemed, was now best left to fate.

To conclude this part of the story, I will state categorically that as of April 30, 1975, no Viet Cong or NVA unit had gotten into any city in the delta, including the remote district capitals, and we were still in firm control of our area. Only on May 1, after we relinquished control, did the enemy dare come out to the highway, and even then they did so with extreme care and concern.

Col. Tran Van Phuc before reeducation, *left*, 1973, and after reeducation, *right*, 1988

Col. Tran Van Phuc *(left)* and Col. Edward Metzner *(right)*, 1967

Col. Tran Van Phuc and family in Kirkland, Wash., 1996

Col. Huynh Van Chinh
before reeducation, 1973

Col. Huynh Van Chinh after reeducation, 1988

Col. Le Nguyen Binh, 1974

(Left to right) Colonel Metzner, Mr. Le Van Hoi, Alina Metzner, and granddaughter

Father Joe Devlin and Maj. Gen. John Murray, defense attache, Saigon, 1974

Colonel Metzner and Father Devlin, 1996

(Left to right) Gen. Le Minh Dao, Alina Metzner, Colonel Metzner, and Chung Van Vu, former police chief, Chuong Thien Province

CHAPTER 11

The Lie of "Thirty Days"

Early the next morning, my wife woke me so we could discuss our options. The other side had entered Vinh Long City and controlled all of the government agencies. They did not yet know where I lived. For my part, I did not know how to act, but decided to remain at home awaiting the inevitable orders to report to them.

My heart ached as I looked at my wife and children, knowing how they would be treated by the Communists. The first day, the occupiers announced over the PA system that students should return to school. My children obeyed the order, taking their books and heading off for school. An hour later they came back home, explaining that they had to change their clothes. Students were to wear long, simple shirts instead of the white *ao dai* that the girls had worn to school before. I knew then that eventually they would be forced to give up their studies. In fact, the very next day the school board declared that the children of the "puppet" army and government would not be allowed to attend school. So, my children had to stay home.

On May 2, they announced over the PA system that all officers and personnel of the "puppet" army and government should go and register at what previously had been Vinh Long Sector Garrison Command. I dutifully arrived there and recognized nearly all the officers of the 9th Division and the Vinh Long Garrison. As the Viet Cong knew nothing about administrative management, they relied on female soldiers of the old regime to take charge of the registration. After giving my name I returned home to wait for instructions.

By May 2, some "April 30th Communists" were out with their red armbands, going from door to door selling National Liberation Front flags and pictures of Ho Chi Minh. The term "April 30th Communist" was popularly used to identify people from the hamlets and urban wards who jumped on the bandwagon and joined the Viet Cong after the war ended. These turncoats told us we had to display the NLF flag and place the portrait of "Uncle Ho" in a place of honor in our homes.

When I arrived at home, I found my brother waiting for me. He had come from Saigon to see about my situation, and offered to take one or two of the children back with him. One problem was that the Viet Cong had assigned people to loiter at a refreshment stand across the street from my home to keep an eye on us, to watch for any suspicious activities. Because of this, and all other things considered, I decided that it was best if my brother returned to Saigon alone. That evening, several North Vietnamese soldiers, male and female, were quartered in my house, to sleep and cook right there among us. Their goal was to control all my family's activities.

The next morning I had to go to the Vinh Long Agricultural Service Office to attend a Communist lecture. The lecturers did not know how to speak to people other than to parrot the phrases they had been taught: "You, brothers, are puppet soldiers, a rebel government, evil. . . . You have come here to study to become honest citizens. . . . Americans are imperialists and you are their lackeys. America ran away and you collapsed." And so on. They insulted us in every possible way, after which they commended their side with wonderful words. The cadre lecturer was stupid looking and not well versed in language. He knew only how to insult and blame. He sat on the ground, his pants rolled up over his knees, rolling a cigarette between his fingers as he talked. After two hours of such "education" we were sent home. The routine continued for several days. In the morning I went to "study," then at midday I returned home, where I waited the rest of the day for further instructions.

On May 5, at approximately 3 o'clock in the afternoon, there was a call on the PA system for us to assemble at the Agricultural Service Office and bring along seven days' worth of provisions. Immediately after the announcement, two Viet Cong cadres wearing Chinese pistols came to my home. I went downstairs to see them, and, after a greeting, I asked them to be seated. They declined the invitation.

"You are Mr. Chinh, aren't you?" they asked. "You are E-commander 16, aren't you?" By this they meant the commander of the 16th Regiment.

I replied that I was, and one of them said, "Have you reported for education yet?"

When I responded that I had, he continued, "Are you prepared for seven days of study, as announced by the provincial delegate?"

I told them I had clothes and money and could go at once.

"Very good," he said. "Then go there for a few days, and you will come back. There is nothing to worry about."

I thanked them, and after they went outside, I kissed my wife and children.

"Stay here and take care of the children," I whispered to my wife. "They say it will be only a few days, but I don't believe them."

I hugged and kissed each child, crying. My wife, too, was sobbing. My children looked at me and said, "Try and come back soon, huh, Papa? Don't be long, okay, Papa?"

I felt like I was dying inside, since I knew it would be a long time before I would come back to see them. My children were young and did not really know what to expect. Without further hesitation, I took a small motor scooter to the appointed place. As I left my house, I noticed two people watching to see if I was really going, or if I might try to make a run for it. Only when they saw that I was heading in the right direction did they leave their post.

Now, twenty-four years later, as I sit and write this, the tears still come. I have to quickly wipe them away so that my wife doesn't see me and also suffer from the memories.

At the assembly point, we were loaded onto military trucks and taken to the Vinh Long airfield a few kilometers away, where there were rows of barracks already full of prisoners who had been brought in since morning, or the day before. They were all officers of the 9th Division and civil officials of Vinh Long Province. It comforted me a little to see those men from my old units, knowing we decided to remain and share the same fate. They greeted me with shouts, perhaps thinking that with their former boss with them in prison, they would be less forlorn.

I visited with some of the men. We even shared a drink or two from a bottle someone had smuggled in. Depression started to overwhelm me, yet I remained resigned to my fate, firmly now being caught in the snare.

Sometime later, I fell asleep, but soon awoke abruptly to the screech of a siren. After quickly packing my few belongings, I joined a line that was forming in the yard outside. The guards called roll and ordered us to board some aging military trucks. The entire camp was evacuated. The time was 1 o'clock in the morning, and I remember there was a half-moon in a clear, starry sky.

As the convoy began to move out, we wondered where we were being taken in the middle of the night. The trucks circled around with no apparent course. After a while, we found ourselves at the rifle range. Someone asked me, "Brother, why are they taking us to the airfield's rifle range?" I was frightened, too, but reasoned they would not transport hundreds of men out just to shoot them all. I thought perhaps the drivers did not know how to reach the highway and had just gotten lost. Thus, I was relieved to hear one of them remark that they had taken a wrong turn and had to go back.

Eventually, we were transported to the Vinh Long jail. I recalled that during the French period the colonial government had built the prison next to the palace and military camp so as to more easily control the inmates. The jail was situated in the town square and had once housed Communist prisoners and criminals. Now it opened its doors to welcome us.

We prisoners were led two by two to the cells. More than one hundred prisoners were packed into my cell, which had originally been constructed to accommodate perhaps forty people. There was barely enough room for us to lie still, and we could not turn or move. We had one small latrine, and it took until morning for everyone to have a chance to use it. The summer weather was hot, and without mosquito nets we formed groups of three, taking turns swatting mosquitoes while the others slept. We sweated profusely, but had to endure it, and eventually we fell asleep from sheer exhaustion.

Early in the morning, we were awakened and made to gather in the yard. A room captain was assigned to keep order and communicate the cadres' instructions to us. Once dismissed, we went to clean up and rest. A few men were selected as cooks to help prepare the food. The Viet Cong were not really organized, so that for several days we had a lot of time on our hands. It was a painful time, during which we pondered our fate and the well-being of our families.

Since my wife was rather innocent in the ways of the world, I was very concerned about her. I was sure she worried about me too, making certain the children never realized her fears. Friends and relatives dared not come to visit her, for fear of repercussions. It was only a half-hour's walk from my home to the prison, but we had no contact with the outside. Those within could not go out, and those outside could not enter. And so, my wife and I remained ignorant of each other's plight.

When we were ordered to turn in, the guards never forgot to remind us of our position, taunting us and cursing and denouncing the "American Imperialists" along with the "puppet army and government." In our cell, we elected individuals to act as cell officers and recorders for our dealings with the Communists. Sometimes the younger prisoners praised the Communists and denounced our side, wanting to appear enthusiastic toward the Party in the hope that such behavior would get them released sooner.

One morning, a cadre ordered all high-ranking officers to a small room we called the "office," where we assembled when they wanted to talk to us in a group. The cadre coldly ordered us to sit on the ground. This man, the district commissar of Vung Liem, carried a pistol and looked like he could eat us alive. He gave us each a piece of paper on which we were to write down our past activities. When we turned in our reports, he denounced them as lies. "Your declarations are false!" he cried. "All your lives you worked to harm the revolution and tried to kill us!" He demanded to know which of us was Bui Van Ba, the "hoodlum" district chief of Vung Liem, Vinh Long Province. Maj. Bui Van Ba stood up and identified himself. The cadre went on wrathfully: "Where have you hidden your sergeant in charge of district intelligence? Why didn't you bring him with you to report to the revolution?" Major Ba replied with some consternation that the man in question had fled. The cadre dismissed us and left angrily, half of his apparent goal of locating these two men and exacting revenge on them temporarily stymied.

Later, we were informed that we had packages from our families. We were anxious, not for the supplies, but for news of our loved ones. My name was called, and I was handed a parcel after confirming that the sender was my daughter. Inside were sticky rice cakes, bananas, and a salty duck egg. I cracked open the eggshell and found a small note that read: "Mama and the children have gone to live with Mama's family." I had known that sooner or later our house would be seized, but the truth struck me hard. I prayed that my family would find peace and not become lost while now having to take care of themselves.

We remained in the Vinh Long jail from May 5 to June 15, 1975. Then the senior officers were transferred to a camp in Military District 9, located near the airfield at Binh Thuy-Can Tho. Ironically, the South Vietnamese government had previously used the camp as a reeducation center for officers who had committed crimes.

As we were being driven away in trucks, civilian buses drove along beside us. We called to the passengers to relay messages to our loved ones, telling them that we were going to the prison in Can Tho and asking them to come and visit us. Out of pity, the bus drivers and passengers signaled their agreement to help, for they knew who we were. Although they did not dare to speak up, their stealthy nods and glances clearly revealed their good will.

Departing Vinh Long City, I looked around at places I knew, now seemingly abandoned. Where was everybody? We passed my home on Nguyen Hue Street, the main city street. The Viet Cong had turned it into the headquarters for Ward 2. I looked at the familiar gate, a pine tree, a mango tree, a plum tree, but my loved ones were gone. My eyes hurt, and I could not look at it any more.

At the new camp, I saw many men who were familiar to me, men of all ranks from the delta provinces, brought here since the beginning of May. It felt good to see my old friends who had not fled, but now came together here. The new prisoners settled in and went straight to the area reserved for families who had been allowed to visit. Looking for someone from Bac Lieu, where my wife's family lived, I saw the wife of an officer friend. I asked her to inform my family of my whereabouts, and to tell them how very much I missed them.

All that day I visited my fellow prisoners. We greeted each other, smiled, and shared our bitterness and suffering at being trapped like animals. At night a clanging sounded, indicating it was time for us to turn in. We organized ourselves into teams of five, appointed room leaders, team leaders, and so forth, and took our designated spaces in the room.

The next day I again went to the visitors' area. It was a stirring scene, seeing many people I had known over the years, those who had been under my authority, those of similar rank and position, yet only a few generals and commanders. Prior to April, 1975, MR IV had had six generals: Gen. Nguyen Khao Nam, commander of MR IV; Gen. Le Van Hung, the assistant MR IV commander; Gen. Chuong Dzenh Quay, chief of staff; Gen. Mach Van Truong, commander of the 21st Division; Gen. Huynh Van Lac, commander of the 9th Division; and Gen. Tran Van Hai, commander of the 7th Division. Generals Nam, Hung, and Hai sacrificed themselves on the night of April 30 and Generals Lac and Hung were imprisoned as I was. Only General Quay escaped in 1975.

During those early weeks, the activity schedule was rather lax. The Communists were not well organized and apparently did not have the prison system adequately planned. In addition, they were afraid that their prisoners might become agitated to the point that they would try to escape. It would not have been difficult for someone to slip away from the camp and, once on the road, make a getaway by hailing a Lambretta minibus. Despite this, we prisoners felt it would do no good to risk our lives, or those of our families, by fleeing. Besides, we had been assured over and over by the Viet Cong that in one month we would be released. Although that deadline was now well past, the Communists denied they had ever made such a claim. "The revolution told you to bring provisions for one month. After that, the camp will take care of your needs. No one said you would be going home in a month." They added, "Those of you who learn well will be released soon. You will not be in education beyond the time set for those who were in the puppet army."

My wife and three of the children came to visit me in an emotional re-union. "Last night," my wife said, "a stranger came and told me you had been taken to Can Tho. We left early today, afraid you would be waiting for us." Like them, I, too, was quite moved, but did not dare cry openly, for fear the guard would send my family away. Some others had been warned by the guard, "What are you crying about? You should be happy to see them. You act as though the revolution is mistreating them!"

After we found a place to sit down, I asked what had happened while I was gone. My wife told me about the family. After I was taken away, the youngest children were afraid to leave her side, and they all slept together in one room. Meanwhile, the Communists took over the lower floor of the house. My wife and children were not allowed to leave the upper floor except to use the kitchen. They even had to ask permission to go to the market for food. When they did leave the house, they were watched and often checked. My wife packed away my military photos and buried my case of medals. She had planned to burn all my papers, but our son Phuoc suggested some of them might be needed at a later date, so certain papers were saved, including birth and marriage records.

The soldiers swaggered in front of them, wearing revolvers and making comments intended to get some kind of reaction from the family. My wife ignored them, playing dumb lest they catch her in a compromising statement and make more trouble. The Communists confiscated the scooter and jeep, and left the family with just a bicycle.

After about one month, my family was ordered to turn over the house to the revolution. At first, they were told to leave immediately, taking with them only the few belongings they could carry. However, my wife asked if they could wait until morning, since they would have to travel far to reach her family in Bac Lieu and there were small children. The soldiers agreed.

Among the Communists in the house was a young woman who demanded to see how much cash the family had. My wife had saved five hundred thousand Republic of Vietnam piastres, about one thousand U.S. dollars. At that time the Viet Cong still permitted the use of South Vietnamese currency. The woman was disappointed, since this did not amount to much money, but she still took four hundred thousand piastres and left my wife the rest. Fortunately my wife had foreseen this possibility and concealed the few other valuables we had by sewing them into the children's clothes in anticipation of the time when they would have to leave.

The next morning, my wife loaded a small truck that her sister had rented, taking two racks with pots and pans and a mix of old and new clothes. A female soldier tried to inspect the children as they were about to depart, when the one in charge said, "That's enough. They need to leave early."

"Oh, *anh!*" (oh, dear!), my wife cried, "by the love of Heaven and Buddha, they confiscated only our house and furniture, cars, and the things inside the house, and so took away these material things. If they had found and taken the jewelry, surely the children would have gone hungry." She wiped her tears as she spoke. I listened in helpless grief and tried to comfort her.

On the road to Bac Lieu, the family picked up two North Vietnamese soldiers looking for a ride. Since there were no seats, the two sat on either side of the hood. The vehicle was stopped at a checkpoint, but the North Vietnamese soldiers prevented the local VC guards from searching through the family's goods for anything they could take. "This sister has had all her property appropriated by the cadres in Vinh Long Province and was permitted by the local comrades to take these remaining possessions to the countryside. What more do you want to look for?" The guards reluctantly allowed them to pass. My wife and her sister heaved a sigh of relief, and silently murmured thanks to Heaven and Buddha, along with a prayer that they be protected for the remainder of the journey.

By evening, they arrived at Bac Lieu. Exhausted, they fell asleep at once. The next day they set up house in the family's chicken coop. The shelter was covered by nipa fronds and walled with sheets of tin. This miserable place was to be their home for a long time.

She told me about the sad end of Maj. Bui Van Ba. About a week after my arrest, the district commissar of Vung Liem had angrily beat him to death. Throughout the day we shared confidences and advice. It was so emotional a reunion that we forgot to eat the food she had brought along. Past midafternoon, I told my wife it was time for her to go because of the long trip back. Taking the bags of food, I returned to my room and wept.

The next morning prison activities began. Although we did not have land and fields for prison "labor," the Communists had found small pieces of land around the camp for us to plant vegetables. In the meantime they kept a careful watch on us and tried to keep us busy so that we would not have time to plot against them.

A routine developed—labor by day and meetings at night after our meal. One clever strategy of the Communists was to generate division among the prisoners. We had heard that if we learned our lessons well in prison, we would be released sooner. Believing this, some men sold out and cooperated with our captors, even to the point of hurting their friends. Eager to gain their captors' praise, some men reported on the others. The competition for better treatment led to jealousies, and the reporting brought about ill feelings and recrimination. One officer, who had once commanded an armored squadron, had the honor of becoming the driver for the camp chief. This officer drove the cadre to his home in Vinh Long and brought back mechanic's tools to repair camp vehicles. He worked his heart out hoping the revolution would not confiscate his property, but they did not release him. Once this man reported me for pausing during the day to chat with friends when I was supposed to be gathering tools. I was called in by the cadre, who sent me to perform hard labor with the others.

The camp was rather crowded, and all the prisoners were field officers or of higher rank. In the midst of the thirty-six barracks, there was one particular cell, isolated from the rest, that was occupied by a white man. I don't know if he was an American or of another nationality. Each morning he carried a small basket of excrement past my room on his way to clean up. No one was allowed to ask questions about him, and he was always guarded by a North Vietnamese soldier. Later he was transferred away from us. Another prisoner, also in separate confinement, hanged himself. I do not know what happened, but only saw others burying his body.

On another occasion, my wife brought the whole family along to visit me. My oldest children, between the ages of fifteen and eighteen, understood the significance of what was happening, but the younger ones were still bewildered by the crowd. I asked my wife how she and the kids were getting along and how they were being treated by the local authorities. She explained that she and the other wives of officers were being called in to meetings by the Communists. "They tell me that I have to go along with their ideas. According to them, a colonel's wife should understand more than the others. Oh, *anh,* all they do is curse the 'puppet' army and government, saying that I lived a privileged life, exploited others, made money off the people, tried to kill the revolution, and so on." It was difficult for her to keep her feelings inside when they blamed and accused her.

She explained that everything was rationed, and all purchases, no matter how small, had to be recorded. The rice was mixed with husks, old and rotten, which they had to buy with sweet potatoes and jicama.

Every once in a while, someone would check on them to see if the family had anything that could be seized. Any excuse was used to justify property seizures, which were performed with a phony display of legality. The Communists would come to a house with notices from kangaroo courts they called "people's courts," authorizing officials to confiscate the goods of people referred to as "bourgeois compradores who exploit the sweat and labor of their compatriots." In one case, the Bac Lieu police chief went to the home of a jewelry store owner just before sunset. Police piled out of the car and drove the family outside without letting them take anything. The police chief had the owner kneel down and bow his head to the ground as he listened to the court's order, calling him a hoarder and speculator who became wealthy off the blood and bones of his compatriots. Instead of the death penalty, which he allegedly deserved, he would be treated leniently and have all his property confiscated. The police then searched the entire premises, dug in the yard, looked under the house, and broke open the walls to see if there was anything hidden. Then they took everything, leaving the victims without even a house. Valuables that were seized were not fully reported. A witness recorded, "For every ten measures of gold they took, they only reported five to their superiors. Of the five they reported, they substituted half with fake gold and kept the rest, complaining that southern gold was no good." People had their goods supposedly recorded officially, then they were beaten and robbed of everything. Many business families committed suicide. During this time, the people of Bac Lieu could not rest, never knowing when their turn would come.

There was little I could offer my wife other than some words of comfort. The time she was with me went by quickly, and she encouraged me to keep up my spirits and my health. It was getting late, so I told the family they had better be on their way back home. I truly wanted them to stay beside me forever, to hold them back, but in the end I had to let them go. As I watched them leave, it felt as though my heart were being cut with a knife.

Prison food consisted of rice confiscated from storehouses along with some jicama. We also had salted fish brought in by outside contractors, who happened to be relatives of the camp guards. Sometimes we had rotten fish or dried squid to eat. But those prisoners who received food from their families did not have to eat dried fish.

One thing that greatly touched me was how every evening several children, aged ten or younger, would come to our tables begging for leftover food. They told us their fathers had been arrested and their mothers could not support them, so they went begging. My heart ached, and I thought of my own children. The Communists would not let my wife work, and when all the family's money was gone, my children would perhaps become like these.

One day we were on our way to gather bricks to pave the roads, and had to cross a cemetery where the dead from battles had been buried. Someone pointed out the resting places of the MR IV commander and his assistant. I stood before the graves in silence a moment, remembering those heroes who would die rather than surrender. Then, sadly I continued to push my three-wheeled cart filled with bricks back to the camp. My colleagues in Can Tho also told me about the Chuong Thien province chief. The Communists took him to the heliport in the city and held a "people's court" right there, forcing the citizens to participate. As they read the death judgment, the brave colonel cursed them so badly they had to force a lemon into his mouth to shut him up. He was executed, and his body was thrown into the jungle. Likewise, other officials, military and civilian, were dealt this same kind of vengeance by the Communists.

One day in June, 1975, there was a big explosion. The fire was so intense it lasted for days and made the nearby asphalt road expand and crack in places. The cadre explained that someone had escaped and destroyed the munitions storage facility at Binh Thuy.

In August, 1975, all officers of senior rank were transferred to a facility near the Communists' headquarters in Saigon. Although this was still a prison, our hope was that with the whole world watching, the Communists would be more careful and not allow anyone to exact personal revenge against any of the prisoners. Luckily, before we left I met the family of one of my friends and asked them to pass on word of my transfer to my family.

On the appointed morning, we left in a convoy of trucks accompanied by North Vietnamese soldiers and cadres. The route took us into Vinh Long City and down Nguyen Hue Street. I was apprehensive. Almost despite myself, I took another look at my former home, not knowing if I would ever see it again. There was one brief moment of sadness, then it was gone.

As we passed familiar places, the people along the roads glanced at us with pity, surely recognizing that this was a convoy of prisoners, officers of the former regime. Yet, they were cautious because of the armed guards with us.

The man in charge of the convoy called a stop at Ben Tre, "to bring the evil enemy colonel province chief along with us." When he came back we were told that the person in question was being held by the people for execution. A story that I later heard related that one morning this former province chief was being taken under guard to the airfield for execution. On the way, the executioners encountered a convoy bearing Madame Nguyen Thi Binh, the foreign minister for the Southern Liberation Front, who was on her way out of Saigon. She asked the senior cadre what was going on, and he explained that a prisoner was going to be executed. "Unless headquarters has so ordered," she retorted, "it is forbidden to execute any more puppet soldiers and administrators. Take him back to prison and await further orders." This story was related by some who had shared a prison with the former province chief at Gia Trang. He had asked him, "Who would have thought that Madame Binh would be giving me a new lease on life?"

The trip took several hours with long stops along the way, and all the prisoners were becoming tired. For all we knew, we were being taken out to be killed. When it started to rain, one of my colleagues whispered, "Heaven sees us suffer and cries in pity." I smiled and replied, "Pray that we should escape this sad plight."

The rain continued to fall as we arrived at the new camp, which I eventually learned was Long Giao, in Long Khanh Province. As we stiffly climbed out of the trucks, we were greeted by the prisoners who had already been there for some time. We all appeared to be of about the same rank, and I figured there were about 375 colonels in the camp. As before, we were processed, assigned to our quarters, and informed of the camp rules. After we had been divided into groups of about forty, group captains and room captains were designated. I was told that there had been some female officers there prior to our arrival, but they had been taken away.

CHAPTER 12

Long Giao Prison

In our new routine, we awakened every morning at five, then exercised for thirty minutes under the direction of one of our members who had specialized in physical fitness and athletics in the army. After breakfast we attended classes. For labor, we took turns cooking, chopping firewood, and toting water, with each room [a large dormitory or barracks crammed with fifty to several hundred men] taking care of its own needs. Food was supplied by contractors and included fish and vegetables.

Each new day followed as the last. We attended "classes" where we listened to the Communists curse and criticize the "puppet" army and the "rebel" government. They said the "American Imperialists" were leeches with two suckers—one to suck the blood of their own people, and the other to suck the blood of their colonies. They repeated these things over and over, lessons they had memorized and parroted from the top ranks to the lowest. It was all they knew.

After the evening meal, we were gathered in meetings to review the day's activities and conduct self-criticism. One of our tasks was to select those who had been "outstanding" in labor and study. Some prisoners continued to believe that we would soon be released, while most did not. My room captain believed it, and even suggested that we ask our families to send us dressy attire so that we would look good for our release ceremony. Still, the anticipated one-month deadline had already passed, and nothing had happened. One high-ranking visiting cadre remarked, "You will study no longer than the time you were puppet soldiers. And if you learn well by that time, you will go home." What a thought—some of us had spent more than twenty years in the service. I myself had been in for twenty-one years. Was that how long I would have to stay in prison? And how did one "learn well"? Even when we went along with the cadres, they still said we were no good, so we never knew what would satisfy them.

In classes, they talked about democracy and encouraged us to speak freely. In truth, they only wanted us to criticize ourselves and make accusations against each other. They hoped we would inform on one another. Those who held a grudge against someone for things that had happened before the war ended could revisit their grudges and turn them into denunciations. Their plan was to tear us apart so we would be easier to manipulate.

It was strange to me that my colleagues often confessed crimes right in front of the rest of us. The cadres told us that all of us were guilty of one crime or another, whether it was being a soldier against the revolution, supporting others who fought against the revolution, maintaining equipment to facilitate the fight against the revolution, or whatever. In short, everyone had crimes to confess, and everyone had to confess his crimes. As childish as this seemed, we had no choice but to follow this mental manipulation, since they were the ones with the guns. Some months after I arrived, one prisoner was given a release notice and was even issued dry provisions for the trip home. This stirred some hope in the rest of us, but it proved to be short-lived. The release order was quickly rescinded, and the prisoner remained with us for another thirteen years, until 1988.

One Sunday they led us out to a munitions storage facility to arrange the disarrayed shells. There were live M79 shells, hand grenades, and artillery shells lying scattered inside the warehouse. We knew that one false move could kill us all, so we worked with extreme care. In late October, we were ordered to gather our belongings and were shipped out at night. Around two in the morning, we arrived at a new camp closer to Saigon. We later learned it was Camp Suoi Mau-Tam Hiep.

Suoi Mau–Tam Hiep

It was an expansive camp covered with barracks overflowing with prisoners. The camp had been used during the war to hold Communist prisoners being transferred from Phu Quoc Island for the heralded prisoner exchange. The roof of our shelter was made of tin sheets; the foundation was cement. There was nothing for us to sleep on, and each prisoner was allowed only about a half-meter of space in which to lie down.

The prison compound was divided into several sections, each enclosed by fences to keep the prisoners apart. I was quartered in the central section, Camp A. On one side was a section for generals. The camp headquarters lay facing us, behind it was NR I from Saigon to Long Khanh. All the soldiers from MR III and MR IV were being detained in this prison camp.

There were two young men in the camp who were clearly mentally disturbed. One of them had wandered away from his home on April 30 and gotten lost. He ate whatever he found along the way, whether dirty or clean. As the day drew on and it got cold, he came upon a uniform discarded by a fleeing ARVN major, so he put it on to keep warm. He was seized by April 30th revolutionaries and taken to the local authorities, who sent him to prison without further investigation. The other mentally disturbed prisoner said his name was Maj. Gen. Le Loi—the name of a famous Vietnamese hero of the fifteenth century and the founder of the Le Dynasty. Both of these men were sent north with my contingent of prisoners. I remember that while I was still in Suoi Mau-Tam Hiep, a cadre asked the ARVN officers if they knew a Maj. Gen. Nguyen Hue, the name of another Vietnamese hero of the late eighteenth century, and they responded there was no such person in our army. A few months after those two unfortunates were taken north, they were released there under local cognizance.

Sanitation was terrible at our camp. There were never sufficient sanitary facilities for the numbers of prisoners there. We relieved ourselves in ditches that we dug ourselves. This attracted swarms of blue flies that completely covered every tree and bush surrounding the latrines. Eventually, mass cases of dysentery broke out. The only thing that prevented many prisoners from dying was the American medicine that families sent their husbands and other relatives, for the Communists gave us nothing.

The cadres told us that our study was now over, and that we had been sent to the camp for labor. We followed a simple routine. Each morning we fixed breakfast from whatever provisions our families had sent us—they were limited to sending three kilos. After that, we were taken out in the yard, where some prisoners planted vegetables, and others used wood to smooth the ground alongside the buildings. The soil was sandy, so whenever it rained the sand became pocked and uneven. A few of us not yet placed in labor teams were assigned by room captains to cook or chop wood.

The Communists were afraid we would discuss matters, share information, and plot against them, so they had strict rules against fraternization. However, since it was so crowded, they couldn't really do much to stop it. We spent our spare time playing Chinese chess and talking about old times. Some of the men gathered pieces of aluminum from antennas to make combs, or they flattened the metal and carved pictures of animals on it to keep as future gifts for their wives.

One night we heard explosions around the perimeter of the camp as machine guns blasted from the guard towers. This went on for several hours.

Dirt and broken bricks flew around and landed on the roofs. Meanwhile, the guards surrounded the barracks and ordered us to stay inside. The next morning we were informed that some prisoners had tried to escape during the night. However, we knew the whole thing had been a staged performance intended to deflate our morale.

Around December, 1975, we were resting at midday, when suddenly we heard gunfire by the gate. The guards rushed over and ordered us inside. We were told that some prisoners had tried to escape. One was shot; the others were caught. They had been allowed outside to work the camp's forge, where we made tools, and now they had abused the trust given them and tried to get away. The captured ones were placed inside connex boxes.

Food and fuel were brought into the camp by hired contractors. Most of the food was old and stale. Some of the rice came from China and had been buried in food caches during the war years. The items the contractors brought in were of poor quality. We could not blame the contractors, since there was no other way they could make money. Since all the prisoners in this camp came from the higher levels of the southern regime, the guards couldn't afford to lose any of us. Any death or escape was reported to their superiors, then fully investigated. The Communists from the north were afraid that their southern counterparts were corrupt and could be bribed into letting some of us go.

As Christmas approached, the Communists expected that the Christian clergy among us would try to organize religious ceremonies, so they took extra precautions to prevent this from taking place. Prisoners were not allowed to gather in groups. Guards closely watched over us and ordered us to turn in early, as others patrolled outside the barracks, eavesdropping to find out if we were up to anything.

Still, the Christian prisoners were determined to celebrate the holiday. I recall how a few ministers discussed this, but one was afraid to take part, believing they all would be caught and punished. Another responded, "If anyone is afraid, he can go back to his room. As for me, even if I should be tortured or killed, I will prepare to welcome our first Christmas night in a Communist prison." On Christmas night, the clergymen assigned men to stand watch around the buildings in case any guards should be seen nearby. Inside, the priests went around to each Christian prisoner by candlelight and conducted a small, private ceremony. If a warning was sounded, they would lie there together and wait for the all-clear sign. Meanwhile, the guards found the night air chilly and did not pursue their assignment too diligently because they wanted to get back quickly to their rooms.

Though simple, the ceremony was solemn and had a profound effect on those who participated. Even those like myself, who were not Christian, were moved and inspired by the courage of the clergymen. The next day, when the cadres tried to get information from us, we just answered that we had gone to sleep early.

That January it was quite cold. We heard that in the north the temperature had dipped to eight degrees Celsius, and many animals had died. This was later confirmed when we were taken to the north. Some rangers captured during the war from the time of President Ngo Dinh Diem told us this, adding, "Heaven is punishing them. They do bad, so they receive bad." The government told our families to send us warm clothing and a little food.

At Tet, the lunar New Year, our captors organized a celebration for us. On Tet Eve, we were allowed extra food, specially prepared for the holiday, including stir-fry with noodles, soup, dried pork, and a few other foods. That night, many of the prisoners got stomachaches because the food had not been properly cooked. Fortunately, my family had sent me some Alka Seltzer tablets, which I shared with some others. The three days of Tet went by rapidly, and we soon returned to the practical realities of survival in prison. I thought about my family and the wonderful Tet celebrations we had enjoyed in the past. Now, struggling to have enough rice to eat and thinking about me in prison, they could hardly enjoy this season.

One day in March, 1976, an unusually large number of guards arrived, and there was tension in the air. The guards told us to select a representative from each room to attend a military court for three prisoners who had been caught trying to escape. Concerned for their fate, we could do nothing except pray that they might somehow avoid the anticipated death sentence. I was not one of those chosen to take part in the mock trial. Those who did attend returned to camp in stony silence. Later they described what they had seen.

The room representatives were assembled in the yard, then led out to bleachers where they sat and faced the accused. The three prisoners were bound to posts set in the middle of the field. They were blindfolded and gagged with lemons in their mouths to prevent them from uttering curses. A judge was present to give the appearance of legality, and there were certain formalities. The charges were read. The prisoners were accused of being reactionaries, trying to escape so they could plot against the revolution, and all manner of false allegations with no word spoken in their defense. Then, three guards fired a volley of shots that tore up the bodies of the hapless prisoners. If this was intended to frighten us, it failed, since after that more prisoners attempted to escape.

Time flew, and we were losing hope of ever seeing our families again. The rainy season only made us more melancholy. May arrived, marking the first anniversary of my imprisonment.

CHAPTER 13

Sent North

In June, 1976, things changed. On June 13, some of the prisoners in my rank were taken away. Three days later, I was among the next group chosen to go. We were taken in about twenty trucks and led away under armed escort. The guards made quite a fuss this time, and surely if any of us got away, there would be hell to pay. When we saw we were being taken to Tan Son Nhut Airport, we realized this was going to be a long journey. We were led aboard two C-130 transport planes and handcuffed to the seats. Under armed guard, we headed north. After hours of flight escorted by MiG fighters, we finally saw the jungles and mountains of the north below us. We landed on an airstrip between two mountains. Caves served as hangars for MiG-19s, presumably from the war when the Americans had bombed the north.

As we disembarked, two cadres welcomed us with the words "Do you know where you are? This is the socialist north. You are here to study and reform for a time to become honest people. Then will the government show you clemency."

They loaded us into covered Molotova trucks and took us away. The road was in very bad condition, and the ride was difficult, especially for those among us with injuries. Instead of following flat roads, we drove through the jungles, uphill and down, twisting here and there. By 4 o'clock that afternoon we came to a town with a market. When we got out of the trucks to board a ferryboat, the local civilians, who lined both sides of the road, shouted curses at us, calling us puppet soldiers, cannibals, and so on. The guards drove them off, saying, "Do you see? The revolution treats you well and protects you. These people would kill you if we weren't here to stop them."

There was a colonel among us who had been a platoon leader during the war against France. He recognized the place where we were as Au Lau Ferry on the Red River. Indeed, the Red River seemed the color of blood as it whirled around beneath us. Our boat was so crowded we hardly seemed to be moving, and with the water's motion we thought we might sink. Eventually, we did make it to the other shore, which turned out to be Yen Bai, famous in our history as the site of an uprising against the French by nationalists.

Four Molotova trucks were waiting for us. They took us about ten kilometers over dirt roads to a large clearing with many barracks. This was to be our new home. As before, we were divided into groups and assigned to sections of the camps. Our temporary sleeping place was a buffalo stable put in order for us by South Vietnamese rangers captured during the war. All the sleeping boards were made of bamboo or other wood from the jungle. The next morning we were transferred to a row of sturdier buildings with brick walls and tile roofs, hastily constructed by the rangers.

Yen Bai Camp 1

We higher-level officers were taken to Camp 1, located near the compound's headquarters. The quarters assigned to the generals lay behind ours beside a hill planted with tea trees. There was also a row of barracks made of bamboo and jungle trees near the brick buildings for the colonels, as there were nearly four hundred of us. Group 776 (a fictitious designation, to prevent the prisoners from knowing the real names of the units), part of a NVA infantry division, was responsible for managing all the prisoners from what had been South Vietnam. We were divided into five compounds, each consisting of ten to fifteen camps of three hundred prisoners. In the mountains of Yen Bai, to the region adjoining China, there must have been altogether eighty such camps, because there were eighty mailboxes, from AH1 to AH80. I counted ten divisions in my camp compound. We were located in the maquis of Yen Bai, about twelve kilometers from the town of Au Lau.

After being organized and instructed in the camp's regulations, we were put to work felling trees in the jungle and cutting thatch to reinforce our lodgings. Our primitive housing was overcrowded. The spaces we each had were only half a meter wide per person, just enough to turn over when we lay down. Nights were very hot, so we often had to spread a cover outside to sleep under. Even when it rained, we slept through it, thoroughly exhausted from the day's work.

At first, I was assigned to the green-vegetable group, planting things such as beans and cabbage to supplement our meals. My job was collecting night soil, which was mixed with water and used as fertilizer. I eventually requested a transfer to another, harder labor group. A friend and I had been carrying baskets to the latrines to carry away the waste. There were only two latrines for four hundred men, so the containers were covered with flies. Faced with this unsanitary situation daily, we lost our appetites at meals. And there was the humiliation—the two of us carrying baskets and using sticks to pick up waste along the road for several kilometers. Each evening, I witnessed a former colonel who had been police chief in MR IV carrying a stick on his shoulder and leading a buffalo. It was painful to watch, but such is the fate of prisoners. The generals were nearby, so we often saw them gathering tea. The Communists would not let them go far from the camp, for fear they might try to escape.

In the months preceding our arrival, the cadres had poisoned the minds of the local people against us. Whenever we passed villages and hamlets, the children threw rocks at us, and the adults cursed us, calling us blood-thirsty cannibals. The cadres and guards pretended to be sympathetic to us. "Look at that!" they'd say. "The people hate you. It would be a bad situation if we weren't here to protect you."

The buildings were not locked then. We turned in at 9 o'clock as cadres patrolled the night. If we needed to relieve ourselves, we were expected to announce, "Cadre, sir, I am going to relieve myself," even if there was no one there to hear us.

One prisoner was Col. Hong Son Dong, who in 1958 had been appointed by Ngo Dinh Diem, then the president of South Vietnam, to the important position of eastern sector chief when the sector was under military command. He was the only prisoner to be released. I heard that during the war between the Viet Minh and the French, his mother had hidden Communist Party leader Le Duan, or someone equally important. We were not sure that that was the reason for his release, but his going caused us to wonder if we too might be released soon.

While at labor, I observed a white man running an electrical generator. His Vietnamese name was Nam, and he was forbidden to have contact with the reeducation prisoners. We were told he was a Cuban sent by Castro to assist Vietnam. This did not make sense to me, since the northerners would hardly need a foreign expert to run a small generator. I suspected he was an American POW. Once as I went by a brickyard where rangers were working at a furnace, the prisoners pointed to a corner of the trees and told me that a few days before our arrival the Communists had transferred out a number of Americans. These Americans had carved their names on the trees there during their lunch breaks.

Food in the north consisted of jicama mixed with rice and flour. The government provided only half of the supplies needed for the prison camps, so we had to devote our energy to growing vegetables and raising livestock. Every morning we were given a steamed wheat roll about half the size of a tennis ball, at noon and in the evenings sometimes two partly filled bowls of rice, other times a roll of tennis-ball size. We had boiled vegetables picked from the jungle to supplement our garden vegetables, which we usually ate with salty water mixed with drinking water. On Communist holidays we got buffalo meat, each person receiving a piece three-fingers wide, and we laid the skin out to preserve to eat later.

Two months after my arrival there was a prison break. Four colonels from the infantry, air force, artillery, and administration had planned it carefully. They asked a friend of mine to join them, and he came to me for advice. I discouraged him from taking off with them, reminding him that we were unfamiliar with the lay of the land. Besides, the jungle was dangerous, and the locals were trained to be on the lookout for strangers. Since there was no fence around the camp, that meant the Communists were confident we could not get away. My friend agreed, in turn trying to get the leader of the escape group to give up the idea. But the leader was young and hardheaded. So, one day as we returned from labor, one team was very late. The guards were quite upset and called us all out for a head count. We learned that the four conspirators were missing. We were told that the prisoners could not get far, and that the guards would not need to go in search of them, because the local people would soon capture them. That night, teams of citizens carrying torches lit up the mountains. Twenty-four hours later, the prisoners were brought back, apparently having been savagely beaten. Only the leader, who had had martial arts training, had resisted. He was a brave man, but he lacked the patience to endure imprisonment. It seems that about three kilometers out they had come to a stream, but one of them could not swim. They traced the length of the water, looking for a place to wade across, but were caught.

In retaliation, the Communists had us dig four holes up in the mountain. The holes were just deep enough and wide enough for a man to stand in. We laid planks across the top and covered these with dirt, as though burying the men alive. The escapees were shackled in these holes night and day, and were let out only to relieve themselves. They were not given blankets or nets to keep off insects or to protect them against the daytime heat and nighttime cold and dampness of the ground. After a short time, the three prisoners who were not battle trained could no longer stand the punishment. They confessed everything and were released to hard labor. As for the leader, he was found hanged, although we thought the Communists had beaten and strangled him, since we knew he had not been allowed to have anything on him with which he might hang himself. For burial, the Communists simply placed him on a mat deep in the jungle.

Afterwards, we were issued only water, salt, and rice for each meal, and we were not allowed to preserve small bits of rice for later by drying it. All medications we had received from our families were confiscated, and, with the utmost vigilance, the guards regularly inspected prisoners' meager private property.

Camp 3

In two months, we were transferred. Luckily, the new camp was only about six kilometers away, since we had to carry our personal items to it. The camp, called Coc Camp, or Camp 3, was situated at the bottom of a valley surrounded by mountains. Perhaps they thought it would be a more difficult place to escape from, and they therefore would have more absolute control over us. Prisoners with the rank of lieutenant colonel or lower went to Camp 1, where we had been earlier. We passed each other along the way as we made the transfer.

Time went by slowly, but the seasons relentlessly followed each other. Winter again approached. We were now instructed to write our families to request food and warm clothing. Northern winters, painfully, were much colder than in the south, and we never could become acclimated to the change. Our captors gave each of us two blankets and a thicker shirt. We had to ask our families for socks, shoes, and hats. But each of us was allowed only one three-kilo package from home per month. Local wards in our home districts were permitted by Communist decree to add another three-kilo package each month, so families that needed to send more requested that the wards help out. Despite a direct and explicit government order to comply, the local cadres used the emotional circumstances involved to elicit bribes under the thinly veiled pretense of funding the added bureaucratic processes. In the end more hardship was placed on already multi-layered obstacles to the fundamental survival of the families.

There was one row of buildings used as an infirmary for the many afflicted with serious illnesses. The only medicine available was an old, traditional one called *xuyen tam lien,* made from the heart of lotus seeds and considered for centuries to be a remedy for almost every ailment, including our problems of diarrhea, fever, cough, flu, stomachache, external and internal infections, and even cancer. Of course, the little green pills provided no relief, no improvement. The illnesses persisted and worsened, and if it were not for the Western medicines sent from home, more of us would have died there. As for doctors, we had only those who had been arrested and brought up from the south, who did their best without adequate and effective resources.

As time went on, we were able to educate the villagers who had previously cursed us, by sharing with them some "capitalist" cold and cough medicines, along with cookies and candies we had received from home. One time, when we were going out to labor, we passed a village where the children had always previously thrown stones at us. This time, the villagers were cordial. During our lunch break, the children came to ask for treats, and the adults asked if we could give them any medicines. Some of us were carrying a few of the precious items with us, and shared a portion of this treasure with the villagers, all of whom were very grateful. Some days later when we returned, they happily remarked how well the "American Imperialist" medicine worked! Afterward, they were happy to see us and often asked to trade with us.

Once, I contracted a bad case of diarrhea and feared it turning into the dreaded dysentery, which out here meant certain death. A number of prisoners had, indeed, been taken ill with a terrible case of the local dysentery, and were subsequently left to die without ceremony or mourning in Yen Bai. Worried and confused when my problem did not abate, I went to the infirmary for treatment. One fellow working there had learned to treat all illness using ancient and traditional methods. He got me to lie down on my back, then he rolled up a piece of paper and lit it on fire. He moved the flame over my stomach to drive out the illness. A friend of mine fortunately caught sight of this "medical procedure" and quickly rousted me out of there. He took me back to my room, inquired about my sanity, and checked around to see if anyone had any legitimate antidiarrhea medicine. He found some, and about an hour after taking it, my problem began to moderate, beginning a long period of recuperation.

We encountered some interesting people in our area. One day we were pushing a "progress cart," a two-wheeled cart with two tongues in front for people to pull, while two others pushed from behind. We brought it past the Au Lau Ferry landing to collect sand for construction. At lunch break, I entered a civilian's house to ask for cooking water. The house, situated on a low hill and surrounded by fruit trees, was barely livable. The owner was polite, directing me to the water and firewood. He was ten years older than I and said he was from a family of village officials from the time of the Nationalist regime. In 1954 he had declined to move to the south, so he had been exiled to this remote spot.

On the way back, we met several old men herding buffalo for their cooperative. They were wearing the long coat of the French and saluted us in military fashion. We exchanged a few words, and discovered they had been noncommissioned officers in the French army, having gone to France during World War II to help fight against the Germans. They had been exiled to Yen Bai since 1954, when the Communists took over the north, and they were not allowed to return to their native homes. This gave us some chilling idea as to what our own final fate might be.

Being in the jungle, we were able to pick wild vegetables and fruit to supplement our diets. Still, it was quite dangerous. The logs we cut were heavy and cumbersome and had to be carried several kilometers down the mountains. Should we lose our footing, we could fall and become injured or die. With two prisoners lifting on each end, we carried the logs back to the camp, which was quite far away, while our guard impatiently urged us to go faster and cursed each time we collapsed.

Most prisoners wanted to be among those who were allowed to go into the jungle to work and subsequently get extra food, but some who did so contracted food poisoning and died. Once, my team was allowed to go out to pick some wild vegetables to supplement our inadequate diet. We normally boiled them a few times and then poured out the water in order to wash away any harmful substances. This time, though, we were really starving, and we immediately ate too much of the vegetables and even drank the water. We became ill, threw up, had bowel-searing diarrhea, and had to immediately struggle to the infirmary.

When we first arrived, we planted jicama, and in a few months it was ready for harvest. Every day now, we had three meals, a small jicama for breakfast and a two-thirds mixture of rice and jicama for both lunch and dinner. We were not allowed to do any individual cooking, but we sometimes were able to throw some pieces of jicama into an aluminum container and cook it without detection. It was never completely cooked, so we would often get dizzy and sick with stomachaches and more diarrhea. At this point, we didn't care, because hunger overcame every other thought, desire, or consideration. In such a situation, the bigger men lost out twice. They had to eat the poorly mixed, insufficiently nutritious food, and were also expected to perform the heavier labor.

One night a friend of mine could not sleep and was moaning in hunger. I gave him a piece of jicama I had been hoarding, and he was able to sleep after that. From then on, I tried hard to secret away a few pieces of food for such purposes. Unless there was some pressing work that needed to be done, we were now permitted to rest on weekends. We used this precious time to bathe when water was available, mend our clothes, or maybe cook and set aside a few pieces of food.

It was quite cold that winter of 1976, the temperature falling at times below zero degrees Celsius (thirty-two degrees Fahrenheit). We had to wear layers of clothing, including boots, gloves, hats. We dug fire pits in our rooms to keep us warm at night. Things finally began to get warmer in the early months of 1977.

Camp 4

Because of overcrowding in the camp, in July, 1977, about 190 prisoners were moved to Camp 4, located three miles away. My team was among those transferred. Once there, I asked to be assigned to the vegetable group. This was less dangerous and less laborious than the jungle assignment, but we had to dig furrows, carry night soil, and tote water for the gardens. Food rations were reduced for this team, and we were given only fifteen kilos of food per month, as opposed to the twenty-one for those chopping trees. Because I had an injury in my right shoulder, I was approved to be given the lighter assignment. Day followed day, the work always the same—digging, planting, carrying fertilizer, and watering the plants.

Another Tet went by and another spring followed. In June, 1978, all the colonels in Camps 3 and 4 were called out. The head of Group 776 explained that his unit had completed its role in our guidance and now we had to move on. He did not elaborate as to where we were going or who would be in charge of us, or if we might be released. But when they told us to gather everything we needed on a daily basis, I knew we were going to another prison. On the last day before moving, we stopped and took time to tend the grave of one of our colleagues who had died at this camp.

At Compound 1, there was a large cemetery to accommodate the many prisoners who died, too often from medical neglect. Beside a lack of adequate medicine, another cause of many of the deaths was the fact that the camp clinic was situated a good distance away and serious cases had to be carried to it in hammocks over rough roads. As a result, some of the sick and injured died along the way.

One night in mid-June, 1978, we set out in a rainstorm on a two-mile trek through thick mud and muck to trucks that would transport us to our new camp. The darkness was so deep we had to grope our way, often dragging our belongings in the mud, sometimes tossing things away in despair. Many men fell, and some had to be carried the remainder of the way. It took nearly six hours for the last of us to complete the walk and climb onto the trucks that awaited us.

The trip took us over the Thang Long Bridge, which had been built during the French colonial period and was the longest span in Vietnam. We continued through Hanoi, even passing Bac Mai Hospital, which news reports had said was destroyed by American bombing during the war. Our convoy traveled on toward Ha Dong Province, another thirty kilometers from the capital. Eventually we came to a wide area surrounded by high walls. Armed soldiers in khaki uniforms stood on both sides of the road. Signs told us this was the Ha Tay reeducation camp, which someone identified as a prison camp run by the security police of the Ministry of the Interior, rather than by the military. I later learned that half of the trucks in our convoy had gone to a reeducation camp in Nam Dinh.

Ha Tay Camp

The officer in charge of Group 776 handed us over to the security police major who ran Ha Tay Camp. In front of the prisoners, the officer reported that the army's duty to reform us had been fulfilled and now he was turning us over to the Ministry of the Interior.

As in previous camps, we found this site had been sectioned off according to military rank. I was taken to the section reserved for colonels. There was a separate section for generals, another for penal prisoners, and an area for lower-ranking officers. A row of meeting rooms and a wide assembly yard formed the center of the camp. We were given food and drink, apparently a ritual for new arrivals. Then we were led to our rooms and locked inside once roll call was completed. The buildings were made of bricks of lime and sand, not cement, which seemed to be in short supply in the north.

The next day, individuals were assigned to be room captains and team leaders. I had the misfortune to be selected leader of my team, one of two in a room of seventy-five prisoners. In this position one walked a delicate line: if I did not do exactly as the guards told me, I would get into trouble; if, however, I did what the Communists wanted, my colleagues would resent me. I decided to avoid the assignment by feigning continuous illness. It was better to be a regular team member and just do what you were told. The work teams in my room were given the tasks of brick making and farming. Work began almost as soon as we arrived at camp. It was the middle of summer, and the heat was unbearable. We often soaked our clothes in water and wiped ourselves down with them to help make the weather tolerable.

After several weeks of hard labor, we were taken off the workforce and ordered to begin writing our life histories. The cadres stated that our memories should still be lucid, and therefore we were to report all aspects of our private lives, what we knew, and who had been working for the Americans. Our accounts were examined weekly by a cadre from the Ministry of the Interior, who criticized the content or complained of our taking too much time. In fact, some of the prisoners dragged on writing their accounts in order to stay off hard labor for as long as possible. We wrote hundreds of pages of endless detail; some of the men even wrote more than a thousand pages. Much of the time, however, we were not really writing. In the morning we set out paper and ink as though preparing to write, then when we were left alone, we cooked and rested, keeping an eye out for our captors, who would constantly ask why we were taking so long.

Toward late 1978 we heard rumors of trouble between Vietnam and China. One day in September, we were visited by Gen. Tran Quyet of the Ministry of the Interior. He informed us that the Chinese had moved several divisions to the border and were poised to strike. When he surprised us by asking for our opinions, some of the prisoners hoped to curry favor by supporting the Hanoi government's stance against the Chinese. Many of us, though, secretly prayed the Chinese would successfully invade and capture Hanoi. When someone asked if we prisoners could volunteer to fight the Chinese in return for a reduction in our sentences, Gen. Tran Quyet declined, saying, "Thank you for your offer, but we don't need you." A week later the general returned and confidently proclaimed that an invasion would be turned back and the Chinese annihilated by nuclear weapons that the Soviet Union had given Vietnam. He went on, "China threatens us by boasting they will have breakfast in Beijing and lunch in Hanoi. The Soviets respond that they will breakfast in Moscow and enjoy lunch in Beijing!" This was meant to infer that should the Chinese dare invade Vietnam, the Soviets would counterinvade.

In February, 1979, two generals and five colonels were transferred to Bac Thai Camp, which was a day's ride north of Hanoi, and we were informed that soon more of us would also be moving. Our future looked bleak, as we seemed again to be left to suffer a slow and withering death. After the Chinese invaded, however, those in the camps in their path were forced to withdraw, among them those of Bac Thai, whose prisoners were sent back to their previous camps. The rest of us were subsequently not transferred.

A few days each month, we were sent back to labor. Once, on our way back to camp, we had a rare chance to talk with some of the local farmers. Their conversation saddened us. They had hoped forces from the south would come to liberate them from their poverty, but now they realized they would have to live that way for the rest of their lives. The image of one old woman sticks in my mind: small and bent, so frail she wouldn't sink if she fell in the water, wearing patched clothes, and carrying a small hoe on her shoulder, she had to work, she said, otherwise she would die of starvation.

We had begun to think we might be allowed to sit and write our life stories until we were released, but once the border situation quieted down, the Hanoi Communists established a team of thirteen senior officers and civil servants from the prisons who had specialized in army engineering and construction. They were to research the building of a huge camp in the mountainous region bordering Laos near the valley of Dien Bien Phu. It seems Le Duc Tho had a plan to exile prisoners there with their families for the remainder of their days. Fortunately, this plan was abandoned, and I heard some guards say that the reason was that the Soviets did not wish to provide support for the plan, even though most of the work was to be done by the prisoners themselves. Perhaps, as well, Hanoi was afraid the Chinese would attack again and liberate the camp.

Ha Tay Camp was kept in good condition because it was used as a model camp for foreign visitors. In late 1979, a delegation from France visited us. The guards had us spruce up the place, especially the section for those, such as family members, who were now allowed brief visits with the prisoners. The Communists wanted to impress the French, so Ha Tay Camp was to be an example of Hanoi's benevolent attitude toward its former enemies. Prior to the visitors' arrival, we were instructed as to what we could say and could not say. Half the prisoners in each room were taken away to make it appear there were only forty people to a room, rather than the actual seventy-five. Scenes were staged so that prisoners were seen strumming guitars, or playing table tennis or volleyball. The kitchen was cleaned and better food was prepared for the prisoners for this one day. In the clinic, patients were given two containers of milk to display—but not to drink. Any infraction of the guards' instructions would result in severe punishment.

On the day of the visit, we were awakened at dawn, and most of us were sent out to labor so we would not be around when the visitors went through the campgrounds. This particular visit seemed to go according to plan. The guards even allowed one prisoner to ask the delegation to deliver a letter to his wife, who was a French citizen. That prisoner was eventually released, because of his wife's advocacy in France.

In 1980, a delegation from Amnesty International came to camps in Ha Tay and Nam Ha. As before, the Communists tried to trick them, but this time there were some slipups. The visitors were skeptical of the scene of content musicians, volleyball players, and book readers. One patient in the clinic took a chance and drank some of the forbidden milk in front of the delegates. He later avoided punishment by claiming that his action was necessary to show the guests that he was being well taken care of. Meanwhile, some reporters who accompanied the delegation remained inquisitive and asked why there were seventy-five sleeping mats and towels in rooms that were supposed to be holding only forty people. After the team had departed, one reporter came back, saying he had left a camera behind. He met us on the road as we returned from labor, and he understood that we and many others belonged to the camp and had intentionally been kept away during the visit.

When I had completed my life history, I was sent back to labor. Most of us were made to plant rice. It was amazing how backward the north was. They didn't have enough buffalo to pull their plows and had to rely on human power to haul the heavy blades through the wet, thick, clinging earth. Most crops turned out poorly, too, because they did not have decent fertilizer.

In early 1980, the Ministry of Defense ordered the senior officer prisoners to write compositions about military tactics involving helicopters, infantry armored personnel carriers, and infantry-armored battlefield coordination, and we were allowed to collaborate with the generals in this effort. This was an unusual move that the camp officials were not happy about, but they could not go against the orders of the Ministry of Defense. Against their will, they also had to give us some better provisions so we could accomplish the task with clear minds.

We continued writing for the Ministry of Defense until 1983. At that time, we had not finished, but when I and some other prisoners were transferred to Nam Ha Camp, the whole project stopped. Hearing that we were to be transferred, we were pleased, even though we had no idea where we were being sent. Eventually, we were told that we were to go to Nam Ha Camp and that Ha Tay was to be used to house corrupt cadres.

Between 1978 and 1983 several colonels died suddenly. Col. Phan Duy Quan of the 9th Infantry Division died in his sleep. Col. Nguyen Van Hoc of military countersecurity, who had come from Hoa Lo to this camp, died while eating dinner, as did Col. Nguyen Van Ton of the armored corps and Col. Ton That Dinh. Col. Pham Khac Tuan of the Bureau of Military Training died from eating spoiled food.

Nam Ha Camp

This time, our transport vehicles were not covered, and we could see the surroundings as we traveled to the new camp. We were also permitted this time to take all of our belongings with us. Since we departed early, we arrived at the new camp by noon and were assigned to empty barracks. Once settled, we ran over to the other barracks and visited old friends. I met one lieutenant colonel who had been a classmate of mine at Thu Duc Military Academy and was in the same unit with me after graduation. As he greeted me, he offered me some wine. How, I asked, did he get hold of this? He replied that this was wine country, and the camp staff had allowed the prisoners to purchase a thousand bottles of wine during this past Tet. I couldn't believe what I was hearing. They could drink, but were punished if they became drunk and disorderly. He took me to the place where the wine was kept so I could see that it was true. Equally as amazing, the prisoners were even able to buy pork.

One young fellow who had been with the special police in 1972 recognized me and came to greet me. To be honest, I did not remember him, but he knew who I was. In this camp he was one of those involved in the bartering, and got away with it because he shared the items received with the guards. For one eighteen-karat gold chain, he bought me several kilos of pork. That the camp permitted such goings on had nothing to do with enlightened humanitarian concern; rather, it was simply a profitable enterprise for the camp commander.

Although things were more relaxed with regard to food and drink, we were kept very busy during the dry season. There were a thousand prisoners, but only two wells and a dry pond in front of the camp. If we wanted water, we had to use bowls and rice cups to scoop up each drop that flowed from the ground.

One morning about a month after our arrival, the guards came down to our quarters and herded us out into the yard. Experience told us we were again going to be transferred. Names were called off, and some of us were sent to a set of barracks set apart from the rest of the camp. The whole thing took about three hours. My good friend and I were among those to be moved. We were pleased to be going anywhere as along as we got away from Nam Ha Camp, with its depressing, surrounding limestone mountains. We said farewell and comforted those left behind.

CHAPTER 14

Return to the South

The very next day we were taken by truck to the train station at Phu Ly in Nam Dinh Province. This time the Communists did not conceal our destination, and told us we were going back to the south. The guards used this opportunity to try to buy our belongings as cheaply as they could. I sold a few of my things to have food money for the journey.

At the station we were handcuffed in pairs. My friend was bigger than I, and he purposely selected me as his partner because my wrist was small and I could slip it out of the handcuffs, thus relaxing our hands. The wait at the station was miserable. The place was not large enough to accommodate hundreds of men, and there were no restrooms. We tried sleeping inside, then outside, where the early seasonal rain dampened us.

At 11 o'clock at night, a train from Hanoi arrived. We boarded in pairs, still handcuffed to each other. Our spirits were light, as in this case we were not afraid of going to another prison. Exhausted, we slept wherever we could find the space, in the seats, on the floor, in whatever position we could manage. We slept through the night, only awakening in the morning to find out where we were. The train was pulled by an old Czech-built engine that barely chugged along. We slept again through the next night and looked out the following day. It was on the second day that we crossed the Ben Hai River and entered the south.

The windows were then ordered shut, both to prevent us from trying to escape into familiar territory and to keep the locals from discovering that the train's passengers were prisoners from the south. The following morning, we arrived at a station in Quang Tri. We took a chance and opened the windows when we stopped to see what was going on outside. What a sight! The houses were filthy and decrepit. Word had apparently gotten out that a trainload of southern prisoners had arrived, because a large crowd had come to meet us. The guards had to drive the civilians away and ordered us to shut the windows. Before the crowd was dispersed, some of the people were able to pass sweet potatoes and corn to us, and vendors did not take our money for their goods. This situation infuriated the guards, but touched us deeply.

The train was quickly ordered out of the station because the guards feared the crowd would return and even grow if we stayed much longer. The whistle blew, and as we moved off, onlookers waved to us, surely their hearts with us.

I had heard about Hue, the last imperial capital of Vietnam—its beautiful scenery, the palaces, mausoleums, the people—although I had never been there myself. Now, as the train passed through the city, I stared to see a place as worn down and dirty as any other in my country. Somehow, word had spread again, and people came to see the train, waving to us from both sides. After a stop of only thirty minutes, we were told to move on.

Continuing south, we passed through Quang Ngai, Quang Tin, and Binh Dinh Provinces, stopping briefly at stations along the way. After three days and three nights, the train finally arrived at the Garai station, Xuan Loc District, Long Khanh Province, about sixty kilometers north of Saigon. Still handcuffed together, we boarded security police trucks, which took us to a camp at Xuan Loc called Z30-A, operated by the security people. The site had previously been a base for regiments of the ARVN 18th Infantry Division.

Camp Z30-A

The compound was near Chua Chan Mountain and comprised three camps. Camp A was a model camp where the camp commanders lived. I was assigned there, where we were divided into three or four groups to a barrack, each with a room captain in charge. Each barrack contained prisoners of all military ranks, along with some penal criminals such as thieves, individuals who had unsuccessfully tried to flee the country, military officers who had fled to Guam and then returned, and political prisoners who were involved in the effort to overthrow the government in what was known as the national restoration movement. The Communists made sure there was a mix of us in each group.

As in the other camps, we had a committee to keep order, which accompanied the guards as they opened and shut the gates every day, announced the arrival of visitors, took food to those in solitary confinement and checked the prisoners' quarters for anything "suspicious." This group had the confidence and trust of the Communist guards.

All the prisoners in the committees were selected by the guards. If the "order committee" was composed of criminals, men in the camp suffered terribly. Unlike the war prisoners, whose relatives sent them food and other provisions, these criminals did not receive any supplies from the outside. Consequently, they made life difficult for us, sometimes beating us to get our food. We were kept under close and strict control, and our movements were constantly observed. The security police were shrewd and cruel. They deliberately selected as group leaders individuals who were hardened criminals or low-ranking military officers who were more malleable and more likely to express resentment of higher-ranking officers by mistreating them.

On our third day at Z30-A, we were sent out to plant corn because the Communists had instituted a rainy season corn-planting campaign. The labor here was ten times as hard as in the north because the Communists were attempting to clear and cultivate vast jungle areas in the mountains. The one positive side of being at Z30-A was that we were closer to our families, in most cases only two days' travel away, versus up to an entire month to get to the northern camps.

Because of my old wounds, I was given the task of boiling the group's drinking water. We were sent to labor regularly twice a day, five days a week. While in the south, prisoners who received food from relatives in the United States were healthier and stronger than those who did not receive such supplemental provisions. This benefited the camp because the stronger prisoners could do more of the harder work, and the camp commanders subsequently received praise for treating their prisoners "humanely," even though the camp staff had done nothing in this respect.

Rooms were set up for visiting families, and visitors could bribe the guards for the chance to stay beyond the designated time limits. Because of the importance of the visits, the guards exploited us by rewarding those prisoners who worked harder with the privilege of more family time. The labor performed at this time was so hard that one colonel died from it.

Immediately upon arrival we wrote to our families to let them know where we were. My wife and children came to visit me as soon as they received the news. The guards called me in early from labor to get cleaned up before I met them, to make sure I looked presentable. At first sight of each other, we sat down and wept. I had planned to comfort them, but was too moved to do so. I did not even recognize my youngest daughter, who was only ten years old when I was first taken away. Now she was grown up. Only my youngest son was not with them, as he had fled Vietnam by boat in 1983. He had eventually settled in the United States, where he helped support the family.

The visit passed quickly, and the guard told us it was time for my family to leave. New arrivals were only permitted three-hour visits, while those who had been in the camp longer could have visits for up to twenty-four hours. I told my family not to feel sad, but to be grateful we were closer now. I asked them to come and visit once a month, as was permitted, keeping in mind that eventually we would be able to spend more time together.

I returned to my room with a heavy heart. After storing away the food my wife had brought, I fell into bed exhausted, but could not rest. Some members of the "order committee" came and told me the guard who supervised them wanted some foreign cigarettes that my wife had given me. I gave them some to make things easier for myself later on. At the time I was trying to learn practical Mandarin and English and had some related language books. When the guards and security people wanted cigarettes, they would come and confiscate the books, refusing to return them until I complied with their demand for cigarettes. After two or three days of this nonsense, I threw the books in the trash.

After a few months in Camp A, I asked to be transferred to the carpentry detail. I wanted to learn a trade that might be of use to me when I was released. I also wanted to get away from the oppressive weather by working inside. We built furniture for the guards. One thing that surprised us was that the younger, lower-ranking guards asked us to make altars for ancestor worship or small outdoor shrines on which fruit and flowers were traditionally placed for occasions such as full-moon days or the lunar New Year. The camp leaders, however, detested these "superstitious" religious practices and threw the altars out when they found them in the soldiers' quarters. The young guards would return days later and ask us to make the altars again, telling us not to report to the security police that we had done so.

One of the prisoners in Camp A was a well-known architect who had been arrested for the crime of being part of the dissident national restoration movement. He was a tough-minded fellow who refused to submit to the Communists and perform prison labor, despite pressure and threats. He reasoned, "The government put me in prison, now it must take care of me. If it can't, then it must let me go. I am not going to work for them, not even picking trash!" They locked him in solitary confinement, but at first did not shackle his legs. When this did not move him, they tried a different strategy, inviting his family to come and take care of him. Still, he appeared indifferent to his family's arrival and refused to see them. He even refused to accept the food they offered, though the camp chief himself talked to him. "Go and tell them I have no family," the prisoner said. "Tell them to go home and not return." The offer was repeated, but the prisoner again refused. He would not even write to them. Sadly the family left him there. Whatever food and gifts they had brought for him he gave to us, keeping nothing for himself. "If I eat these things," he said, "they will have control over me. I eat only what the camp gives me." He understood that the Communists were using his family and his hunger to get to him and force him to become more compliant.

Although I admired his heroism and intransigence, I personally believed that trying singly to oppose the Communists in our situation was like banging your head against a wall. Still, each of us had personal, individual ideals, and I did not criticize him, but only pitied one so talented who would surely perish unjustly. This is not to say that I toadied to the Communists or acted as an informant against my fellow prisoners in order to earn my captors' favor. That would have been cowardly and low. Eventually, because they could not move this man, the Communists threw him in a cell and chained his legs, then slowly starved him to death.

My detail was ordered to make his coffin, a simple box of unplaned wood. We tried to make it look a little more respectable, and although our group leader was criticized for our doing so, we offered the guards some presents so they would let us give the deceased a decent burial. Four of us carried the coffin to a three-wheeled cart for transport to burial, and all the prisoners stood for a moment in respectful silence to bid him farewell.

CHAPTER 15

Released

A large number of lower-ranking officers were released early in 1986. The government had found it politically expedient to begin showing leniency. They wanted to impress the American government in an effort to open the way to normalized relations between the two countries. Since Camp B was in worse physical condition, it was abandoned, and its remaining prisoners brought over to Camp A. Among them was my carpentry detail, which had been transferred to Camp B earlier. We planted corn each day to trade for rice. Once a month my family came to visit. Between visits, time passed as slowly as ever, with nothing extraordinary to vary the routine.

On September 2, 1987, the Communists' Independence Day, half the prisoners with the rank of colonel were released. They were elated, of course, while the rest of us were left to sadly ponder why we were not included. I saw that many of those who were released were former province chiefs, like myself, so I began to hope that my time would come soon. It was now hard for us to do any constructive work, and the guards just prodded us harder to continue our labor. From that point on, we anxiously watched for the arrival of security police or their vehicles, which seemed to always preceded a release.

During February, 1988, just before the lunar New Year holiday of Tet, a convoy of vehicles arrived from Saigon and Hanoi. Several days later, we were called in early from labor. As we assembled in the yard, the names of those who were to be released for the New Year were called out. All but a few with the rank of colonel were called, myself included. We heard that those not selected were to be sent to Ham Tan Camp to be confined with some generals.

When dismissed, we returned to our quarters to pack our belongings. Prisoners who had been released before us had been given enough money to pay for transportation back home, although the bus drivers and vendors along the way refused to accept money from them. In spite of how hard life was for them, these fellow countrymen would not take money from those who had been unjustly imprisoned, for now they clearly saw the difference between the old and new systems and understood what we had been fighting for.

Our release was different. We colonels were not simply released, given money, and told to make our own ways home, but instead were to be transported by security police vehicles. As we set out, we were not certain where they were taking us. We became anxious when we arrived in Saigon and headed toward Chi Hoa Jail. Once there, however, we were instructed to board vehicles that would take us to our respective home provinces. I and several others boarded the one headed for Bac Lieu. This was a reformist period for the government, with Nguyen Van Linh the party secretary in Vietnam and Gorbachev the leader in the Soviet Union. Our drivers were listening to a music tape with a southern singer performing a traditional tune called "To Hien Thanh." The song tells of an honest official punishing some corrupt mandarins. One of the guards accompanying us said to another, "Listen to this, comrade, and don't do anything that will put you in prison!" They laughed.

As we headed south, then turned west, I recognized many of the familiar places of my past. We passed, in turn, Phu Lam, Ben Luc Bridge, Long An Bridge, My Tho, My Thuan Ferry, and Can Tho Ferry. On the surface, not much had changed in thirteen years. As we drove past my old house, I strained to see how it looked and what the Communists were using it for. I saw only the shapes of one mango tree and one plum tree.

We did not stop in Bac Lieu, but continued on to Ca Mau Province, now renamed Minh Hai. About 2 o'clock in the morning we turned into an open field and arrived at a place that looked like another reeducation camp. I saw a sign that read Cay Gua Camp. Some of us feared that although the central authorities had released us, the local authorities were now going to confine us longer. We were relieved when the camp's commander informed us that this was to be only a resting spot, as there were no accommodations ready for us elsewhere in the province. I suggested to my companions that we trust the cadre's word and try to get some rest.

We were awakened at 6 o'clock, and about an hour later arrived in town. It was now only a couple of days before Tet, and we were met by a group of province security police and a lieutenant colonel. These men were in charge of keeping track of released prisoners, following their movements, and monitoring their activities. They tried to sweet talk us, asking us not to be resentful or have any ill feelings toward our captors. "The past is past," the lieutenant colonel said. "Everything has its errors. When you return, join with the local people to build the country." We grunted assent to get it over with, and only wanted to get home as quickly as possible.

The next day, a security policeman asked us for our home addresses, allegedly so the district police could contact our families and invite them to our release ceremony. We became quite concerned that night when we were driven to a cemetery and were instructed to stay in thatch huts. After they cooked a pig for us and once again tried to convince us to forget the past, we relaxed somewhat. In the morning we were given leave to visit the city and any relatives who might live there, but were cautioned to return by 5 o'clock that evening.

Three days before Tet, a delegation from Military Region 9 conducted a formal release ceremony. They praised their regime as humanitarian and mouthed other propaganda, after which we were invited to thank the nation and the Party. In conclusion, they informed us that the local authorities unfortunately did not have transportation to bring our families to the ceremony or to take us home. We did not need such assistance at this point and just wanted to get home as soon as we could. When dismissed, a friend and I boarded a bus for home. Every seat was taken, but the riders recognized us as released prisoners, and some of them knew my friend. They greeted us warmly and offered us their seats. The others on board were gracious to us, and the driver refused our fares.

The road was old and in great disrepair, and the drive seemed to take forever. We arrived at Bac Lieu about 2 o'clock in the afternoon. I got a ride from the station in a trailer pulled by a bicycle, the best transportation available under the "progressive" Communist system. We passed the Cao Dai cathedral, and using that landmark, I was able to locate the home of my wife's family. The driver refused my offer to pay and rode off.

My nephews and nieces playing outside spotted me and called to the others in the house, "Uncle is here!" My brother-in-law came to greet me. He had been a junior officer in the rangers and also had spent some time in prison. Then I hastened around back where my wife and children were living, and we enjoyed a tearful reunion.

Despite my happiness at being back with my loved ones, I was ill at ease. Since I was considered an enemy of the state, I was concerned that the authorities might come at any time to arrest me again. Under the Communists, every place was like a prison, but at least now I was with my family and not trapped inside four walls, waking each morning to the clanging of a gong. Many nights in the camps I had dreamed that I had wings and could fly away to a ship that would take me to a free land. That clanging would then wake me from my fantasy and bring me back to harsh reality. That evening, when all my children had returned home, we shared our first meal together in thirteen years.

I reported my presence to the local authorities the next day. Although all released prisoners were supposed to be pardoned, the security police closely monitored my activities and sent "visitors" to check up on me. The family enjoyed the blessing of being together for the lunar New Year celebration even though the house was in terrible condition. The roof was half thatch and half tin and leaked badly when it rained. Posts were propped up in many places to keep the roof from collapsing. It grieved me to realize that my wife and children had been living like this for thirteen years.

After the third day of Tet, the local authorities organized a public ceremony. I used the occasion to thank the government for my release and for allowing me to be reunited with my family. A government representative congratulated me and welcomed me into the neighborhood. The citizens knew my family and our plight, and added sympathy for us to their hatred of the Communists.

All the people in the area seemed to be very poor. One story worth telling concerns a canal that ran for about five kilometers alongside the highway from Soc Trang toward Bac Lieu. The canal was used to drain off high water during major rains and keep the town from flooding. After the Communists took over Bac Lieu, they did not like the way the canal looked, so they forced the citizens living nearby to fill it in, utilizing whatever means they could. The effort took six months. Any family that failed to complete its quota of labor was accused of opposing the government and sent to one of the New Economic Zones. The sweat and tears of the people were wasted on this senseless project, for when the rains came, the town, predictably, was again flooded.

I discussed with my wife the condition of our home, and we agreed that I should go to visit a friend in Vinh Long who could give me some bricks. The trip would also provide the opportunity to go to Tra Vinh and visit the graves of my parents and older brother who had passed away. The nearby office of the neighborhood security group granted permission for my trip, and the officer in charge declared that I was free to come and go as I pleased, although, he added, it would be better to keep local authorities informed in case I should be detained somewhere else.

It took quite a long time to get a seat on a bus. Cadres and soldiers were given preference, and it was common for people to wait half a day to get on a bus. The old buses traveled slowly, and it was eight o'clock at night when I finally arrived in Vinh Long. From there, I took a Lambretta to my relatives' house. Another emotional reunion ensued, and they offered to help me on my mission.

After a night sharing experiences with my family, I took a bus to Tra Vinh. The scenery along the way brought back so many memories I had to shut my eyes to block them out. I only opened them again when the driver announced we were entering the city. The bus station itself had changed little, but the stalls and vending booths surrounding it were in a decrepit state, the result of government campaigns against capitalists and Chinese merchants. Tra Vinh City had once been a very prosperous area, but now it looked depressing.

When asked around for the whereabouts of my family, some children recognized that I was their uncle, and they took me to my brother's home. My brother hastened to inform the local authorities of my presence, being careful to explain that I was there to pay respects to my deceased parents during the Tet holiday. He then purchased roast pork, fruit, candles, and incense for the occasion. At the cemetery, I set these offerings on the altar, lit incense, and prayed. As I lit the candles and glanced at the pictures of my father and mother, I burst into tears. I wept harder at the grave site. I was consoled to see that my youngest sister, who had fled the country and now lived in the United States, had sent the family money to care for the grave. Now, years later, I am still moved by the recollection.

The next day, more relatives came to see the man returned from prison. Neighbors, too, came to see me, since they knew my family and respected us. They inquired about my health, and though I said nothing, my bony frame answered for me. When I returned to Bac Lieu, I reported my arrival to the security police, then went about the task of fixing the house with the help of the children.

Since my release, my son in the United States had been trying to sponsor me to come to America. As I tried to complete the processing on my end, I went from the local security police office to the district office to the province office for emigration, where I met the head of the province bureau for political defense, which was responsible for monitoring any activities that might be seen as antigovernment, including the actions of released prisoners. This official, who held the rank of lieutenant colonel, invited me into his office and offered me tea. After recounting how my son was attempting to sponsor me to the United States, he said, "Brother Chinh, forget the past.

Everyone makes mistakes. The government has shown you clemency and is allowing you to go to America. When you arrive there and make a good living, bring back money to build your country."

After several hours—and several packs of foreign cigarettes I had brought along to expedite the process—the paperwork was completed. From then on my family waited anxiously for the day we could depart, leaving behind an oppressive system of government and enforced poverty, where we were not permitted to work for a living because of our political status. Soon afterward, we heard that the Vietnamese and American governments were negotiating the emigration of former prisoners. A number of us were called back to the province emigration office for processing in the program known as Humanitarian Operation, or HO. After a while, the negotiations broke down. The Vietnamese government wanted to release lower-ranking officers first, whereas the Americans wanted to admit those who had been in prison the longest, regardless of rank. Since the senior prisoners were also the higher-ranking officers, the positions of Hanoi and Washington were extremely opposite, and the talks became stalled. Despite the problems, our hopes were buoyed by the fact that the two sides were at least discussing the matter. We felt that sooner or later everything would be worked out, and the talks did resume in early 1990.

The two sides eventually agreed that former prisoners of mixed ranks who had been imprisoned for at least three years would come to the United States incrementally. The agreement did not expedite receiving my family's exit permit as I had hoped, so I returned through the bureaucracy for further processing, which included payment of a large fee for the paperwork. We were then scheduled to leave in January, 1991, in the fifth increment.

Even though we now had our exit permit and an appointment for an exit interview, my family remained on guard as we waited to go. Experience had shown that the Communists would say one thing and do another, so we feared they might try to find an excuse to keep us from leaving. We would not feel secure until we had set foot on the soil of a free country.

I settled my affairs in Bac Lieu and went to pay a visit to my parents' graves. In Vinh Long I had to clear up the situation regarding possession of our old house, which had been confiscated but was still in my name, and any other possible so-called debts to the state. The cadre representing the province people's committee, which oversaw my case, had been a regimental commander in the Vinh Long-Tra Vinh-Sa Dec area. When he discovered I had been his former adversary as commander of the 16th Regiment, 9th Division, he was surprised at my youth; he himself was then in his sixties. "You became a colonel when you were in your thirties!" he exclaimed. "Well, now we are brothers and both Vietnamese. The past is over. We must look to the future."

These same words parroted by all the Communists did not have a ring of sincerity. I pretended to go along with it, just the same. When the cadre asked me to sign over my house to the province, I remarked that it had already been confiscated by the local authorities and no longer belonged to me either to give away or to claim back. In the end, I received one note indicating that I had no real estate holdings and another that I had no outstanding debts with the state.

I returned to Saigon again for my interview and physical checkup. While waiting, I visited some friends who had already gone through the process in order to find out what to expect. An old friend I stayed with offered to make me a new suit for my journey to America, but I declined, saying it was enough that I had my patched shirt and pants.

Although I tried to reassure and calm my family, we still remained anxious. I gathered together all the documents we had saved attesting to my former positions in the army and as province chief, as well as birth and marriage certificates, and so on. As it happened, the interview went smoothly, because my file was complete. The family was accepted for immigration to the United States, and we were given a flight date of January 11, 1991.

Not all cases were as simple as ours. We met one woman whose husband had been in prison but died after his release. His widow was not sure if she would be granted an interview. Another woman left the office cursing and tearing up her documents when she was denied an interview. She had worked for the Americans during the war, but was unable to get accepted for emigration. Hundreds of families lined up outside the foreign affairs office, waiting for an opportunity to state their case to leave the country.

We returned home to prepare for our departure. There were emotional farewells with relatives and neighbors, and one final visit to my parents' graves. Right up to the end, the local security police, none too happy at our good fortune, kept an eye on us, seemingly looking for an excuse to delay our departure. On the appointed day, we went to the April 30th Hospital in Saigon for our physical examinations as required. We were found to be free of any contagious diseases, although there was some concern regarding images showing up on my chest X ray that looked like signs of tuberculosis. The lung spots turned out to be bone fragments from a wound I had sustained during the war, and so I was passed. After that, we got our immunizations and passports, and packed our belongings.

The day of our departure finally arrived. During the one-hour drive to Tan Son Nhut Airport, I was reminded of 1976, when I was taken there as a prisoner being transferred to North Vietnam. Now, I was leaving my country and homeland, my relatives and friends, and the site of my parents' graves. As I climbed the ramp, I turned and took one last look at those who had come to see us off. It was a difficult parting, but one we had to make for our livelihood and freedom.

The plane soon taxied down the runway and took off. As we rose into the air, we looked out at the country we were leaving behind, a land now governed by repression and deception. Our hearts grew light as we left Vietnamese airspace. We were glad to be leaving and grateful to the United States for accepting us.

Part III

Col. Le Nguyen Binh's Story

CHAPTER 16

Advisory Days

While I never was Col. Le Nguyen Binh's advisor, on each of my four tours in Vietnam we served closely together and were friends. During my first tour, 1964–65, with the Vietnamese 7th Infantry Division in My Tho, Dinh Tuong Province, Binh was the division intelligence officer, and I was the division's psychological warfare (psywar) and pacification advisor. Several months after my arrival, Binh became involved in helping my psywar counterpart and me complete a plan that convinced the division's commanding general to be concerned with the safety and protection of the innocent civilians who were always caught up in the violence of division operations.

Later, prompted by that same concern for the safety of the population of a VC-controlled village soon to be the target of a large division attack, he collaborated with the psywar section chief to accurately profile the village population and underscore their discontent with the suffering and privation caused by the Communists' control. The resulting division operations plan was drawn up with the assistance of the psywar and pacification section chief, a collaboration previously unheard of in the war. Both the battle plan and a clever deception plan focused on getting the villagers out of the way and fooling the enemy into taking an escape route that led them into a trap.

That successful operation stemmed from Binh's adroit analysis of small bits of seemingly unconnected information, which resulted in targeting and decimating the 514th VC main force battalion near a village named Ba Dua, Vinh Kim District. He deduced that the battalion and some smaller attached units had a pattern of movement that cycled them, in roughly predictable timing, through a clockwise series of small base areas. The targeted enemy battalion would, at the time of our surprise attack, be about two kilometers south of Ba Dua.

The battle made rare history in several ways: the intelligence was accurate; the deception worked to protect the villagers and strike the enemy; a VC battalion was severely mauled; and only one civilian was killed, unfortunately, during the lengthy and widespread battle violence.

On my second tour in 1967, I returned to Dinh Tuong Province as province senior advisor to Colonel Phuc, the province chief. Binh, now a major, was still the division intelligence chief. While we did not work together on a day-to-day basis, our mutual interest in the security of the province and the neutralization of the main force enemy units operating there provided periodic opportunity to work hand in hand pursing those objectives.

One occasion, which was of a much less serious nature than was generally the rule, still brings a smile to my face after all these years when I recall it.

The phone rang in my room as I lay in bed reading, tired from a long day walking the rice paddies with Colonel Phuc in Cai Lay. I jumped up to answer, since a call at that late hour usually was from the province operations center, relaying bad news of some incident. The voice of Major Binh surprised me. He apologized for phoning so late, but he was calling a special meeting at his house to discuss something important that had just come up. Could I come? Whatever it was must have been unusually urgent, I thought, as I had little direct contact with the division and with Binh. I replied that I'd be there as soon as I could dress. Binh gave me directions to his house, admonishing me to be sure to come alone and not to tell anybody I was going. When I hung up, I looked at my watch. It was a quarter past midnight.

While driving through the deserted streets, I suddenly wondered if it really was Binh who had called. I thought I recognized his voice, but now I couldn't be sure. Why the caution to come alone? Why the secrecy? Was I getting sucked into something? As I found the darkened house, I wondered if it was even Binh's. Parking the jeep a safe distance away, I drew and cocked my pistol and tried to approach noiselessly.

As I climbed the front steps, the door opened a crack, and Binh poked his head out to make sure of who it was. As I fumbled quickly to put away my pistol, he ushered me inside, where several small groups in uniform were talking. I followed him to where Colonel Phuc and a group of province and division officers were sitting. They all laughed at the joke that had brought me there, and Phuc explained that Binh, a longtime close friend, had arranged the impromptu gathering to help Phuc escape the pressures of the job and relax. Phuc wanted me there with him, correctly guessing that

I would welcome a short period of relaxation too. He gave a large smile as I exhaled deeply and sat down beside him, feeling pleased and honored to be included.

During my third and my fourth final tour, between 1969 and 1973, Binh and I interacted irregularly as a result of the distance between our places of duty. He was the IV Corps intelligence chief in Can Tho City, and a colonel. I was the province senior advisor on three different occasions in provinces of the IV Corps area in the Mekong Delta.

When the 1973 Paris Peace Talks concluded in a so-called cease-fire agreement, which unconscionably stacked the odds in favor of Hanoi and heralded the eventual American withdrawal, we had occasion to get together after several subsequent monthly province chief's meetings at IV Corps headquarters. Although we both intuitively knew that the departure of all American military personnel was not far off, such disappointment was not mentioned in our conversations, which were really only thinly disguised opportunities to express a very difficult farewell. Our next conversation, a much happier one, took place twenty-three years later.

CHAPTER 17

The Dreaded Alert

Early one day during the last week of April, 1975, the alert was passed in our headquarters that confirmed the news that I prayed would never happen. The American government was abandoning my country when we most needed its help. Thoughts flooded my mind as I reviewed the choice of actions I could take and their consequences.

For almost twenty-four years, I had fought and served faithfully and honorably in the army. Most of my assignments were in military intelligence, as was my present duty as chief of intelligence (G-2) for Military Region IV. The region included most of the Mekong Delta area south of Saigon, and I was at its headquarters in Can Tho City, a hundred miles south of Saigon, where my family resided.

The possibility of a disastrous ending for my family and my country seemed incredible. It would be one last ironic circumstance in the many that had shaped my life and forced my decisions. Born in Son Tay Province, North Vietnam, I became a southerner at four years of age when my father, a government agricultural engineer, was transferred to the south in 1935.

When I graduated from high school in 1950, the war between the Viet Minh and the French was raging. Although most youth my age were being drafted into the new national army, I was fortunate enough to complete two years of college before I had to decide how I would serve. In 1952, I volunteered for the Army Officer's Academy in Dalat. The course was accelerated because of the rapid expansion of the army, and I graduated as a second lieutenant in 1953. Since the main battles with the Viet Minh were being fought in the north, I was assigned to a mobile brigade there and subsequently saw action in every following major engagement.

Following the loss of Dien Bien Phu and defeat of the French in 1954 by the Viet Minh, the brigade returned to the south in accordance with the treaty that divided the country. By 1960, I had risen to the position of intelligence officer for the 7th Division at Bien Hoa, north of Saigon. When the Communists proclaimed formation of the National Liberation Front, followed by increased insurgent activity throughout the south, the 7th Division was relocated to the Mekong Delta Tactical Zone and established headquarters in My Tho City, Dinh Tuong Province.

From this period forward, I served in intelligence assignments that permitted me to make important contributions to my country's security, but also served to mark me for vengeance by our enemies. In 1969, I worked at the Joint General Staff Saigon Headquarters for the chief of the Combined Intelligence Center. In 1971, the commanding general of IV Corps requested my assignment as his corps intelligence officer, where I remained until the fateful days of April, 1975. During my career, I attended six various courses in America including two in Okinawa.

All these facts returned to my mind when the corps signal section intercepted messages from Viet Cong and North Vietnamese Army commanders to their units, giving instructions of the fate to befall captured ranking government military officers. I had no doubt about the swift and final "people's justice" that would be dealt to me. But, for now, my foremost and immediate concern was for my family.

When the military situation throughout the country rapidly began to deteriorate, I had entrusted the family's safety to American friends and associates in Saigon. Their assurances of help to get my wife and two sons and daughter out of Vietnam, if the worst happened, had given me the peace of mind to concentrate on doing my job at this critical time.

If ever the decision had to be made, I knew in my heart that I could not surrender since it would mean my death and leave my family to struggle alone. I was confident I could escape, if necessary, but only after assurance of my family's safety. Since the decision when and how to escape would have to be made and executed quickly, now was the time to seek reassurance that my family was, indeed, included in the Americans' evacuation plans.

On April 25, Gen. Nguyen Khoa Nam, the commander of MR IV, gave me permission to go to Saigon by helicopter to attend to my family's needs. True to their promises, my American friends had included my family in specific evacuation plans. At the proper moment, they would be among dependents flown from Tan Son Nhut Airport to the Philippines. We said a difficult good-bye, wondering if it would be our last, and I returned to Can Tho with lingering apprehensions that I still could not dismiss. Would the evacuation work? Even if the answer to that question was yes, would I ever see my family again?

The next day, April 26, brought increasingly grim news of battles on the approaches to Saigon. Our forces were fighting under the heavy handicap of severe shortages of ammunition, fuel, and spare parts. Lack of fresh reinforcements was also preventing us from establishing a defense of the capital in required strength and depth. Although our MR IV units were holding well, if Saigon was to fall, the enemy could then redirect all its strength toward us. It would then only be a matter of time, even though we would make the Communists pay a terrible price for their gains. There was no doubt about our will to continue the fight, and realistic and accurate intelligence was the one vital element I could keep providing that would enable us to do so. Among the increasingly disheartening and confused battle reports, good news came that strengthened my spirit and raised my determination. My family had departed Vietnam and was safe.

Fierce battles raged for three more days. Although the knowledge that we no longer had our allies beside us brought a sadness that surprised me in its intensity, a more powerful thought arose that overcame and replaced the sadness with renewed pride and determination. Vietnam still existed, and the units of IV Corps were courageously fighting to defend it.

Our final day of destiny was April 30. Throughout headquarters, the air was alive with alternating feelings of apprehension and grim determination. As I posted the intelligence map, it was increasingly difficult to keep up with the growing number and swiftness of enemy movements.

General Nam called an urgent staff meeting. He was a very strong soldier who had the respect and full support of all who served under him. We all eagerly awaited his orders, and I had a sense that something momentous was upon us. From my last posting of the enemy situation map, I felt that General Nam's words could not offer much encouragement. The general's opening words repeated a simple message we had heard from him many times before. As good soldiers, we must strictly follow our orders. This time, though, the orders would be most difficult to obey. Our new president, Duong Van Minh, had broadcast a surrender order at 10:29 A.M. It ended, "All generals and military men of all ranks are to observe the order absolutely." General Nam added that we must do exactly as directed, and he would not accept discussion as to any alternative actions.

Although the order was not totally unexpected, it still hit as a shock and disappointment. I was filled with shame, anger, and disgust. I felt that the government had sold out the people and the nation to the Communists. Knowing the enemy so well for so long, surely our leaders must have understood in their hearts that there would be no reconciliation, no coexistence, no compassion toward those who had opposed the enemy.

CHAPTER 18

Escape

Now, it was clear to me that my true duty was to escape. Even if I failed in the attempt, it would bring a better end for a soldier than to meekly surrender and die dishonorably. When I announced my decision to my men, some stepped forward to say they would go along with me.

Our rapid escape preparations were completed around noon. I had arranged for three riverboats to transport our group, which had now grown to about one hundred twenty. About half were civilians, including women and children. One of our group was another colonel who had twenty-two family members with him. Seeing his problem and sensing his concerns, I said a silent prayer of thanks that my family was already safe. While our escape boats were large, motorized sampans made for inland waterway travel only, and were not seaworthy, they would have to do. Our first step would be an immediate and rapid run down the Bassac River to where it met the South China Sea. Once there, we would assess our situation and contemplate our next step.

We reached the coast near eight in the evening without incident. The journey was made with extreme caution and seemed painfully slow. Considering the limited capability of our boats and the unknown hazards of the open sea, we decided it was unwise for us to proceed further at this time. Although many of our group had become increasingly unhappy, confused, and alarmingly noisy, there was no other option but to sit and wait things out in the dark. Our best hope was that a South Vietnamese navy ship, also escaping, would find us and either take us aboard or escort us out, away from the coast. Feeling certain that a number of American navy ships remained close by in international waters, I anticipated that one would find us and pick us up.

About midnight, we heard the distant sound of motors approaching. With a mixture of hope and fear, we remained quiet and waited. The source of the sound was a Vietnamese navy amphibious landing craft operated by twelve navy seals. They were almost as glad to see us as we were to see them, as none of them knew anything about seamanship or navigation. Because the craft was small and two of its four engines were not working, we negotiated how many of us they could take, and then decided who should go. They agreed to take twenty of us and would accept only the highest ranking military officers and their families. Since the other colonel had twenty-two in his family, he elected to remain with all of them in the three riverboats. Nineteen others chose to join me in the landing craft, and we watched quietly as we separated from and lost sight of the others in the dark. I made it clear to the seals that in this situation rank did not matter. I was army; they were navy, and they were in command and control.

After traveling straight out to sea for about half an hour, we met a large sampan containing about forty soldiers. The navy men did not want to take them aboard because we were already fully loaded. I convinced them that we must take the chance because the sampan would surely sink in bad weather. Now we had seventy-five people jammed aboard, mostly military, and most of them armed. With survival at stake, with so many weapons in the hands of men from many different units, and with helpless civilians with us, a long delay would surely bring trouble. We needed to be found and picked up soon.

The next day, with tensions mounting and fear prompting panic, our remaining two engines stopped. All efforts to get them started again failed. As we slowly drifted in the vast and silent sea under a merciless sun, all eyes stared toward the horizon for the ship we hoped would come to deliver us. If we were not picked up soon, difficult decisions would have to be made to prevent trouble and avoid disaster. I called a meeting with an army and a navy representative. We needed to choose somebody to take charge, assume responsibility, and make hard decisions since disorder, panic, or irrationality could kill us all. They agreed and, because of my rank, designated me as commander.

Later in the day, three vessels appeared on the horizon. Not knowing whether they were friend or foe, we prepared for either eventuality. Luck was with us. They were small but sturdy and seaworthy ocean fishing boats. Needing to grasp this opportunity to improve our situation, we determined to use force, if necessary, to seize them. The boats were South Vietnamese and had been out to sea for a long time. The crews did not know of the loss of our country. After explaining what had happened, we were able to board them without violence. Out of fear of the Communists, the fishermen sadly joined our escape attempt. Before turning out to sea again, we sunk the landing craft as a precaution, should the enemy be searching for escapees. There was one compass on the fishing boats. In addition, I had a roughly sketched map that I had made from available charts before leaving Can Tho. With no other navigation aids, I concluded our best destination was Singapore. After some discussion and disagreement, most consented after I explained why I chose Singapore. With my chart and the compass, we could determine and follow a course to Malaysia. Once we sighted one of the Malaysian islands, we could turn south and follow the coastline to Singapore. Once there, we would contact U.S. officials for assistance.

CHAPTER 19

Avoiding Mutiny

On our third day at sea, some men wanted to return to Vietnam. They regretted leaving their families behind in their haste to escape. I told them that if they could get about thirty people to agree to return with them, they could take one of the boats and go. They couldn't find enough to go, and I announced to all that we must then continue on to Singapore together. Whoever wished could arrange to return home when we arrived there. This decision caused many arguments. Because there had been some previous firing of weapons out of frustration, worry, and boredom, I felt that I had to collect and secure all weapons to avoid serious trouble. I retained mine for security and locked up all the rest. Most agreed and helped me convince the reluctant ones to comply. Ammunition was also collected, and hand grenades were thrown overboard.

Our most serious and immediate problem was drinking water. Each boat had two 200-liter cans, about 110 gallons for each boat. By rationing use of the water for cooking rice, plus issuing one-half cup per person per day for drinking, I calculated that our supply would see us through the journey. Again, there was disagreement and argument. After several attempts were made to steal water, I placed guards over the supply. Since I couldn't chance arming the guards, I chose those who appeared physically strong enough to use force, if required.

Our slow progress through a seemingly endless sea under a searing sun began to take a mental and physical toll on everyone. Some moaned and cried all the time; others mumbled prayers. Periodic fights broke out that further strained already taut nerves. After I helped break up each fight, I tried to offer encouragement and foster hope, but deep in my own heart, I suffered my own doubts. My thoughts were constantly of my family. Where were they now? My wife was not strong, and this was the first time she had been out of Vietnam. Could she care for three children in a foreign land?

What were their thoughts and concerns at this time? All I could do was to pray for them and for my survival, so we could be reunited.

One morning, I awoke to find that all the ammunition had been stolen. Luckily, I had carefully hidden away some for my pistol. Sensing that only a very few were guilty and that the majority would support me, I called everyone together. I explained what had happened and threatened to shoot anyone who might try to take any weapons. Inside, I wasn't sure I could do that, but by bluster and a determined voice, I tried to be convincing.

As we awakened on the morning of the fifth day, a ship appeared on the horizon. It looked like our prayers had been answered. As it passed close, we joyfully prepared to hail it and plead for help. At the last minute, we saw it was flying a Russian flag. We then just stood still and prayed they would ignore us as we quietly continued on our way.

Hours later, our spirits were lifted when we saw our first land. It was Malaysia, and for a moment we were greatly tempted to continue on a straight course and land there. The temptation was put behind us after I remembered and explained that throughout our war with the north, Malaysia had remained neutral, supporting neither side. Now that Hanoi had won, the Malaysian government might send us back out of fear of Hanoi and to appease the Communists. We turned south as originally planned, toward Singapore. At least the sight of land relieved some tension and renewed our hopes.

Just before sunset, we met another large ship. It was the *Panama*, flying the flag of Taiwan. They stopped and let me go aboard. They were very good to us and gave us a supply of noodles, rice, oil, and water along with some navigation charts. The captain offered to take us with him back to Taiwan if we would await his return from Singapore. Fearing a lengthy internment in Taiwan, I gratefully declined the offer. For a short time we tailed behind the *Panama* on its way to Singapore, confirming the correct course. It soon outdistanced us in the dark of evening, and we were once again alone.

CHAPTER 20

Singapore

May 6, at nine in the morning, we reached Singapore. A navy boat came out to investigate who we were and requested we turn our weapons over to them before they led us into port. I promised to give them the weapons once we were in port, if they would help us get in touch with U.S. officials. When we did get to port, we were required to stay on our boats because thirty-seven hundred Vietnamese refugees had preceded us there. After receiving water and an offer to allow anyone who was ill to disembark, we remained on our boats for the next seven days. No contact with U.S. officials was permitted.

Hiding my own frustration, I counseled everyone to remain patient and calm. This unexpected and unhappy turn of events convinced thirty of our group to return to Vietnam. They were willing to risk the hazards of the sea and the treatment of the Communists in order to rejoin the families they had left behind. The food and water was divided, we wished them good luck, and said our farewells amid the shedding of many tears. We who remained had to leave our boats and were transferred to a much larger Vietnamese fishing trawler manned by a Japanese crew. The crew objected to receiving us, but the Singapore authorities gave them no choice.

This new situation renewed our concerns and tensions. Showing their resentment at every opportunity, the Japanese crew kept to themselves and refused to help us in any way. Our concerns gave rise to a new plan, one made possible by the availability of the large seaworthy trawler with its competent crew. We would embark for the Philippines, where we would surely meet the Americans and secure their help. Using the two pistols I had hidden from the Singapore authorities, we induced the Japanese crew to depart for our new destination.

Each day at sea, the crew found some way or pretense to make trouble for us. On May 14, two weeks after we left our homeland, they reported major engine trouble. When we investigated, nothing was found wrong. When they sullenly resumed course, I was concerned that they would change course toward Japan while we were asleep. To prevent such an attempt, I organized and assigned two-hour watches to ensure that we maintained the correct compass course for the Philippines.

For three days after setting up the watches, all went well. While our relationship with the crew improved a bit, weariness and fatigue caught up with us, and we relaxed our guard. Before sundown, we happily sighted land once more and looked forward to the end of our ordeal. After midnight, during one of my inspections to ensure that the compass setting remained correct, the land was no longer in sight. A glance at the compass confirmed that our course had been changed northward to bypass the Philippines. The navy seals agreed with me that we now had no other choice but to forcibly take over the ship, which was accomplished quickly and without bloodshed.

At last, on May 20, we arrived off Subic Bay. A U.S. Navy helicopter came out and circled us, acknowledging the Vietnamese flag flying from our mast. A smile and salute from the pilot released the pent-up joy and relief we had been reluctant to express until then. Shortly thereafter, we were escorted into port by a navy ship.

After twenty-one days we could wash, shave, change into clean clothes, and relax. Upon realizing that I was finally free, the depth and intensity of my emotions were overwhelming. Before throwing away my old dirty uniform, I cut off my army insignia and rank. I wanted to keep these small but important reminders that I had served my people and my country honorably and faithfully to the end. Inquiry about my family brought the happy response that they were safely in America. Within days, I was on my way to join them.

CHAPTER 21

A New Life in America

Colonel Binh and his family were reunited in Bellevue, Washington, in July, 1975. Initially sponsored by friends, the family became self-supporting after two months. His wife, formerly a professor at Gia Long College in Saigon, went to work sewing curtains. In 1979, she was hired as an electric cable–testing technician for the Boeing Company in Seattle.

Colonel Binh began by working any odd job made available through a job service center. Later, he worked as a baker for Seattle's largest bakery. After studying drafting for two years, and attending the University of Washington for two additional years, he was subsequently employed as a mechanical designer. Since retiring in 1994, he volunteers as a translator for newly arrived Vietnamese armed forces veterans between time spent reading, gardening, and parachuting.

His oldest son has a master's degree in transportation, is married, has one boy and one girl, and lives near him in Washington. His second son is also married, has a bachelor's degree in fashion designing, and is involved in sport shoe design and design consultation with Nike, Misuno, Elesse, and Avia. He lives in Portland, Oregon, with his American wife and son. Binh's daughter has a master's degree in chemical engineering and works for Boeing. She is married and has one daughter.

Part IV

One a Hero, One a Saint

CHAPTER 22

Gen. Le Minh Dao

Le Minh Dao's lengthy and detailed story is not included here. He is writing his own book, the specifics of which could not be done justice in an abbreviated account here. Nevertheless, some of the facts of who Dao was, what he accomplished, how we met and over the years how our friendship grew and deepened, and finally what became of him need telling.

After spending a month in Cam Ranh Bay hospital, convalescing from a case of infectious hepatitis in December, 1967, I was being released. The pleasure of leaving the hospital was tempered by the news I'd just received that I would not be returning for duty in Dinh Tuong Province. It had been necessary to replace me as senior advisor there because of an alarming increase in enemy activity that made it prudent to have another experienced military officer in charge of the province advisory team.

My new assignment was as province senior advisor in Chuong Thien Province. Because of the same rise in enemy activity in Chuong Thien that threatened Dinh Tuong Province and because the previous province senior advisor had already departed for home, I was advised to waste no time getting there. The hospital library had an embassy pamphlet with statistics and information about all the provinces; I checked it out and read about my new home: "Chuong Thien:—Province capitol is Vi Thanh. Location: 150 miles southwest of Saigon at the head of the Ca Mau Peninsula."

The area has long been a safe haven for the VC. In an attempt to establish control in the area, President Diem had created the province several years ago out of the four bordering Mekong Delta provinces—Kien Giang, Ba Xuyen, Bac Lieu, and Phong Dinh. The latest countrywide security rating placed Chuong Thien last out of the forty-four provinces of South Vietnam. Two days earlier, I had received my combat infantryman badge. Although I qualified for the award by getting shot at in Dinh Tuong, as things would turn out, the badge would actually be earned several times over while I was working with Maj. Le Minh Dao, the province chief of Chuong Thien.

For the next nine months, including the 1968 Tet Offensive, and intermittently for seven years thereafter, Dao and I forged a trusting and enduring friendship. Our relationship grew and expanded with each gain, each loss, each happy occasion, each sadness. Our shared and special closeness was born out of our mutual and relentless desire to obtain a lasting peace with freedom for his people. In our words and in our actions, we considered ourselves as brothers.

During the intervening years following my departure from Chuong Thien, Dao's career rose rapidly, and he continually advanced higher in rank and responsibility. I also moved through a series of assignments that provided increased opportunity to contribute to our goal of a free and secure Vietnam. Whenever the opportunity presented itself, we visited each other. Toward the end of my final tour of duty, he attended my wedding in April, 1973, to the Vietnamese national women's tennis champion. In turn, my wife and I were his guests at the anniversary celebration of the 18th Infantry Division, which he then commanded as a brigadier general.

My last assignment, from February, 1973, to August, 1974, was with the U.S. Defense Attaché Office as chief of the Liaison Section to the Vietnamese Joint General Staff (JGS). In that capacity, I made periodic trips around the country to ascertain or confirm and document the deteriorating military situation resulting from Hanoi's blatant violations of the cease-fire agreement. My last trip was to see Dao.

His 18th Division was approximately fifty miles northwest of Saigon, and the general was being pressed hard by the North Vietnamese. JGS headquarters had told him I was coming, and he was waiting for me outside his heavily sandbagged command bunker when the Air America helicopter landed. After we shook hands, he shouted over the noise of the helicopter engine, "Brother, have the pilot take off and come back for you later. If the helicopter stays here, it will draw enemy fire." I nodded that I understood and asked the pilot to return for me in an hour, but not to land unless he saw me outside the bunker, waving. As Dao led me inside, the low rumble of explosions not far away underlined his concern. I had not expected to find that his command post was within range of enemy artillery.

We spent only a few minutes in personal conversation before he started the briefing. The corps commander was due to visit shortly, and Dao wanted to finish with me before he arrived. Dao did the briefing while his staff sat and listened. The more he described his situation, the madder he got. As he paced up and down in front of the map with his hands alternately hanging by the thumbs in his pockets and waving at or slapping the map, I recognized the old, fiery Dao from Chuong Thien:

"Colonel Metzner, the Communists have me at a disadvantage in every way. My soldiers want to fight and they do well anything I ask them, but the truth is, we are on the defensive. We are rationed to four artillery rounds a day for each gun and about a hundred rifle bullets for each soldier each month—*each month!* The North Vietnamese have an unlimited supply.

My soldiers are being killed and wounded because the enemy's artillery can reach us from beyond our guns' range, and I cannot even move my guns and tanks close enough to fight and fire back because we get so little gasoline."

He hadn't taken his piercing eyes off mine, and now he pointed in the direction of a very close volley of explosions: "Communist artillery units have hundreds of observers in the coconut and rubber trees and fire ten, twenty, fifty rounds at anything that moves. My soldiers remain strong, and their spirit is high, but courage alone cannot stop steel."

I was listening silently and without expression, but inside my heart was wrenched with anger and frustration. When he launched into a scathing tirade against the corps commander, calling him nonsupportive, dense, and uncaring, I was amazed. For him to say this openly in front of his staff meant that he had their absolute loyalty and support and that he was not overstating the seriousness of the situation.

When he finished, Dao hung his thumbs in his pockets and stared silently at the floor. "I understand everything clearly, General," I said firmly as I slowly got out of the chair. "And my report will contain everything exactly as you've told me." That was my official response in front of his staff, but as he waited with me for the helicopter outside the bunker, I slammed my fist into my hand. "Damn it, brother, I'm sorry, really sorry that this is what we've come to. I don't know what encouragement I can give you." As the helicopter landed on the road, Dao cut me off, speaking tersely through clenched teeth: "I know it is bad and not as we hoped. Give us only what we need to fight with, and we will do the dying and get the job done."

Then he gave me his old smile and shook my hand, sending regards to my wife and telling me to take care of myself. I smiled back and added that I wished for God and Buddha to be with him. He returned my wave as the helicopter took off, then turned and briskly strode into the bunker.

Dao's parting words, "Give us only what we need to fight with, and we will do the dying," rang painfully in my ears as our support continued to fade. And I felt a terrible shame in my heart as I looked over the beautiful countryside that, when viewed from the helicopter's altitude and at its speed, looked deceptively peaceful.

In April, 1975, eight months after I returned home, just before Saigon fell to the Communists, I caught a glimpse of Dao on an evening television news broadcast. He was briefing a group of newsmen at the 18th Division command post at the crucial road junction of Xuan Loc, northeast of Saigon. Although his units were heavily outnumbered and outgunned by massed North Vietnamese armor and artillery, it was the old, fiery Dao, attacking his tormentors. Knowing that his division was all that remained between the bulk of the North Vietnamese army and Saigon, Dao led his troops to fight heroically, virtually destroying two enemy divisions before finally being overwhelmed.

Dao rotted in North Vietnamese jails for seventeen years. I sadly had heard that he became blind and later died in prison in 1985, but that was a false report. In April, 1994, through a mutual friend, I learned that he had survived and was in New York City, where I happily contacted him. We were reunited in California in 1996.

Dao was not surprised to learn that I had heard he had become blind in prison. Many people had heard that, and he explained why. During some of his darkest moments, he prayed to God that if he lived through the ordeal, if his family also survived, and if he returned safely to them, he would convert to Christianity from Buddhism. At that time, he thought he was going blind because as a result of malnutrition and stress, his left eye pupil rotated almost completely out of visibility.

Sometime thereafter, a new prisoner was moved into the cell adjacent to Dao's. That prisoner was a Catholic priest. Dao began communicating with him through the small space where the wall separating them rose to the ceiling. He told the priest of his promise to God, and the priest gave him a miniature Bible he had successfully concealed from the guards.

Day by day, as Dao struggled to read the minuscule print in the dim half-light of his cell, the effort strengthened his eye muscles, and the left pupil slowly, over time, rotated back to its normal position. Dao interpreted that as a sign from God and kept his promise to convert after his release, when he learned that his family had safely escaped the country.

CHAPTER 23

Father Joe Devlin

Father Joe Devlin, a venerable Irishman, was obviously not Vietnamese and not a former counterpart of mine. Still, his story belongs in this book, because Father Joe came very close to being considered a Vietnamese saint by the countless people he helped in Southeast Asia through his devotion, dedication, and long service to them.

The full details of his leaving the comfort and safety of teaching at a midwest Jesuit college, seeking a flock in Vietnam, and ministering to them would be compelling and fascinating history all by itself. Unfortunately, when moment and circumstance brought us together for one last visit, time and distance had clouded his recollection of the many extraordinary, humanitarian achievements for his beloved and widespread Vietnamese flock, which he always downplayed as ordinary.

I first met Father Joe when he came to my office in Saigon in the summer of 1973, seeking help for "his flock." The imposing figure who limped forward to shake my hand was an impressive and pleasant surprise. Almost a foot taller than I, he was broad shouldered and large boned but lean as a rail. His crew-cut gray hair and weathered, square-jawed face framed a bright disarming smile above the white collar of his short-sleeved black shirt. When he sat down after crunching my hand in his large, powerful grasp, I saw what caused his limp. His right shoe had a heel and sole that were built up about three inches to compensate for some deformity.

Father Joe was then caring for a large group of mostly Catholic war refugees near the town of Phan Thiet, which bordered the South China Sea about ninety miles northeast of Saigon. Several years before, he had become touched by the plight of the Vietnamese people and the suffering the war had brought, and, feeling unchallenged and unrewarded in his teaching duties, he had asked his Jesuit superiors for permission to seek a flock to shepherd in Vietnam. The Catholic Charities Office in Saigon responded that they would welcome his efforts, and he ended up ministering to several thousand displaced war refugees still caught up in the midst of the conflict.

Before we parted that first day, I made him promise to contact me the next time he came to Saigon so he could meet my family. Father Joe returned five or six times and on each occasion had dinner with us. He and my wife and children took to each other immediately. On each visit, the affection grew.

He made the final trip to see us for a last dinner a week before I left Vietnam in August, 1974, at the conclusion of my fourth tour. His refugee village was under increasing pressure from the VC, and he now had a new concern for his flock. He had to supervise and provide for their security and protection. Alina and I had grown to love the old saint, and we had real cause to be deeply concerned for his safety. Trying to keep the conversation light, I jokingly cautioned that he needed to exercise extreme care because he had to be the tallest target in the country and, with his game leg, probably was the slowest too.

He answered that he would be okay because he had his own weapon now. It was a .45 caliber pistol, the gift of a departing USAID advisor. He was a "pistol-packing padre" now and was becoming a pretty fair shot. The implication that he felt the need to be armed wasn't missed. The children went to bed after giving Father Joe extralong hugs, and we talked until late, delaying our farewells until the last possible minute.

Alina and I walked with him to his new means of transportation, parked in front of the house. It was an aged three-wheel motorcycle that he'd convinced the Pittsburgh Police Traffic Department in Pennsylvania to contribute to his cause. As his white plastic pith helmet bounced down the dark street and out of sight, Alina cried, and I whispered a prayer for his safety.

When Vietnam fell, Father Joe made it out with the last groups of evacuees. He visited us at Fort Ord, California, just before he left to go back to the refugee camps of Malaysia to help bring compassion and aid to the suffering and order amid the chaos there.

Earlier, in May, 1972, the following story by Father Joe had been featured in the *Ogden* (Utah) *Standard-Examiner.*

Editorials
Ogden's Father Joe Devlin Buries Friend; Corp. Joe Cao "Rests Where Heroes Are"

(Of the many letters that Father Joseph Devlin, S.J., has written us since leaving Ogden to establish his refugee mission in the war-torn Mekong

Delta, the following on the death of Corp. Joseph Nguyen van Cao is the most poignant. In contrasting paragraphs, Father Joe writes of how Corporal Joe died and then gives his own thoughts on his 44-year-old South Vietnamese friend.)

1800 hours: The soldier of "lookout" is tense with excitement. In his lofty perch above the outpost of Hoa Binh, his powerful field glasses have picked up one, two, three V.C.! There they are, about a mile away, in the tall grass, making their way toward the canal. He shouts down to the fort "Call Dai uy Nghia! V.C. at 12 o'clock."

Twelve! That was the number in his family when I first met him—himself, his wife and 10 children. In those early days I had no penicillin and his wife was dying of pneumonia. She lingered a day or two, then died. I expressed my regrets at not being able to save her. He smiled—he had the saddest smile I have ever seen.

It seemed to say, "That's OK, you did your best." In the little nondescript burial ground at Tram Chim he buried her. He dug her grave and covered it with his own hands and with his bare feet he stamped the dirt down. Later he bought a cement cross to mark Maria's resting place.

Dai uy Nghia—Captain Nghia—is a veteran V.C. fighter. Now he is atop the tower, peering through the binoculars. No doubt about it. There are at least three V.C. moving toward the canal, maybe intent on setting up booby traps or catching the night watch in an ambush. He triggers the radio communication set, "Attention, Squad Eight. This is Dai uy Nghia."

Dai uy is a good man. Yet when I asked him later for the name of my friend he hesitates. When I asked the parish priest, he, too, wasn't sure.

They did know that he was a member of region force 992, his rank was chief corporal and his name was just Joe. They might have added that 44 years of age was just a bit too old for a guy named Joe to be playing soldier in the marshes of the delta.

About a mile from the village, a squad of six soldiers is sprawled out on the bank of the canal: a lieutenant, Corporal Joe, and the four soldiers. Not quite twilight. Yet there is nothing to get excited about. Free and easy does it! Then the radio sounds forth. Gone is their quiet and composure.

"Free and easy." His life was never meant to be that way. He was on duty there at Hoa Binh when his four year old took sick and died.

Poor little thing. It must have been a loser, too. For when they came for medicine, someone intercepted them and gave them a useless Vietnamese remedy, instead. Had we known we could have saved her.

He buried her there beside his wife, he and I together. He went back to guarding Hoa Binh through the sun and rain. I went back to Tram Chim resolved to keep my eye on the remaining children.

"500 meters due north, three, possibly more, V.C., making their way toward your position. Go get them. Maintain radio contact." The lieutenant improvises a hasty battle plan. Grab your rifle. Bolts click. Safety off. Automatic on. You can't see them but the enemy is there, somewhere, in the tall grass.

"In the tall grass," that's where I'd see him, each time my sampan took me from Hoa Binh to Tram Chim. He'd be one of 60 soldiers stretched out, guarding my life down Ambush Alley. We'd shout a greeting as I passed and that was it.

I remember, though, once as we passed, I wondered with prophetic insight, "Who would I bury next—him or his children?"

"300 meters," the radio warned. "Let each man do his duty."

"Duty!" Duty to one's country. Duty to one's family. Duty to one's self to be a man. He was always doing one or the other with no holidays in between. Like the time during another funeral when I looked over to see him enclosing his wife's burial plot with a barbed wire fence.

"100 meters. You are approximately 100 meters apart. Do you see the enemy?" "Negative that." "Proceed with caution."

The lump crawls into your throat. Your mouth dries, pulse quickens, muscles tense.

What in the name of heaven is a 44–year-old man doing crawling through the grass? Aren't 20 years of war enough? What of your nine children?"

Lord, God of Host, be with us yet. Jesus, if I must die this night let it be with courage and honor. Mary Mother, I commend my children to your care.

"30 meters . . . ," the muted voice whispers. "You are 30 meters apart. Good luck. Out."

Though I walk in the dark valley, my heart shall not fear. A man with a history of tragedy was moving towards his destiny! "Joe, come back, let the younger men take over!" Too late!

The automatic fire of M16's and AK47's break the stillness. He has hit one V.C. It is essential to recover the enemy's weapon, lest it be used again. Get that gun!

He moves forward—and in that moment the hand of God reached out and touched. I'm sure, too, a trumpet sounded in heaven; a great trumpet, loud and clear.

How would Joyce Kilmer put it:

"Go to Sleep, Go to Sleep."
"Danger's past, Now at Last, Go to Sleep."

I buried him as befits a brave man. I buried him in the same faded, green uniform he always wore and in the soil of the land he sought to free.

I dug his grave myself, just where I knew he'd want to rest, by his wife and near his child. Over his grave the last volley rang forth and we left him there with our tears and the flag of Vietnam covering him proudly.

No more those sad smiles. No more walking through the swamps. No more standing guard on a thirty foot-wide canal under burning suns or in torrential rains.

One day I shall return to the cemetery, stretch barbed wire around his grave and place a headstone for a friend. It will read:

Joseph Nguyen Van Cao
Age 44
"His soul now rests where heroes are!"

At the end of America's involvement, another contribution from Father Joe was published in the *Standard-Examiner's* editorial column.

Returning Vietnam Veterans Earned Gratitude of People of S.E. Asia

(Editor's Note: As the U.S. participation in the nation's longest war winds down, a former Ogdenite points out vividly the fact that our returning veterans have earned the gratitude of the people of America and Vietnam. The author is the Rev. Joe Devlin, S.J., Catholic priest at a remote Mekong Delta mission.)

For the returning veterans, there are not proud songs.

The visible presence of war on television, the fury and tragedy of battle have taken away all the calmness from American judgment.

Vietnam, in the American dictionary, is an obscene word. And so the veteran comes home, an enigma to his own, who call him "cruel and ugly." But to the Vietnamese, the American GI is a man of awe and respect.

To an American airport he comes, this man of sacrifice and danger. He will be greeted and welcomed by his wife and children. No flags will be flying.

At a nearby airport gate, perhaps the heroes of the sporting world will be greeted by thousands of fans. Enigma? Who is? The soldier? Or the American people?

"The evil men do lives after them. The good is oft interred with their bones."

My Lai we all remember. Drugs we know. But how many know the orphanages helped by the American military man, the schools they supplied, the poor children. . . .

The soldier helped out where he could because his empathy for people told him it should be done. He asked for no broadcasts, no praise, no blaring trumpets.

Like the mountain climber, he climbed his own mountain because "It was there." For every cheating soldier who dealt with the black market, a thousand were here who did charitable works.

For every My Lai, there were a thousand other hamlets lifted to a better life.

And for every man exposed to dope, a thousand lived an ordered life.

Despite it all, he is "branded" first in war but last in the hearts of his countrymen.

But not last in my heart.

I have been a constant and critical observer of the U.S. Armed Forces in Vietnam. I watched them in their barracks, in their outposts, in their ships, and in their choppers.

I was present at their briefings, watched them at menial tasks, in the camps and in the fields—the young GIs, the sailors, the noncoms, the pilots, the doctors, the officers, the chaplains.

American never had finer representation, not in the halls of ivy nor the halls of Congress. They were the American image of our way of life, and what a witness they gave!

Together we went, the armed soldier and I, speeding down a canal, bending heaven and hell to get a little dying girl out of the middle of the Mekong and to a U.S. Navy doctor.

We were a team. As we three of us fought to keep a little boy's life-breath flowing until the Medevac could finally get there with his big bird.

We saw trips off the flight deck by night to save a little boy and Navy gun ships converted into mercy carriers, threading the needle by night to carry off injured civilians in our village.

Gunshot wounds. Booby trap injuries. Crippled children. The works. The Americans took care of them all!

Shades of Tom Dooley? Rather shades of a deep American compassion and an inbred desire to help the needy and the underdog.

They came in conquest, this army from the United States. But they remained to be conquered by an army of orphaned kids, the needy, lepers and missionaries.

You can learn a lot about popularity from the children of a land. Little naked children would stand in an open hut and say "My, my." (The Americans, the Americans.) Most likely they'd reach out their hands for candy.

To them, he wasn't "cruel," he wasn't ugly. They might not know of their native buffalo, but everyone, everywhere knew the American from over the sea.

San Francisco, Ogden, Hoboken all spelled magic Camelot to the Vietnamese.

I saw only a little of what Americans have done here. I multiply what I say by the thousands—the saving operations of life and limb, the refugees, the lepers, the mountain-people cared for. It was a volume of many-splendored deeds told once but not twice.

The world will wait long before occupying armies ever again behave so circumspectly. One great heritage he leaves behind: "From the soldiers of the Armed Forces of the United States to the people of South Vietnam, bought and paid for by American blood, to you we bequeath Freedom."

Indeed, he cast a giant shadow.

And so he goes, and for his going this eastern world is a little bit less good.

Like the "passing of Arthur," his going is the end of an epoch, an emptiness that will not be filled.

Down deep in the Scriptures, we reach for some words to describe him. *"Erant gigantes in diebus illis."*

In those days, giants walked the earth. And good men, big men, once walked the land of Vietnam.

The little ones they sought to help are still here. The giants are gone, their flag is gone, but their memory and spirit still hovers over the land.

"Good-bye, you great big generous lugs. Indeed, we shall remember!"

After his final return from Southeast Asia in the mid 1980s, Father Joe continued to serve the Vietnamese and Philippine communities at Our Lady of

Peace Church Parish in Santa Clara, California, but never stopped trying to wrangle a return overseas to the needy with whom his heart remained. Such constant requests to his superiors brought responses like this:

> Dear Joe:
> Thanks for your latest note. I was sorry to hear about the delays in getting something lined up. Things do seem very possible for Zambia. We will wait and see.
> As you note, if things do not materialize in the next few weeks we can have a talk about alternatives.
> I recently ran across some verses of interest. I do not think it is very good poetry but it fits you:
>
> Some want to live within the sound
> of church or chapel bell.
> I want to run a rescue ship
> within a yard of hell.
>
> Your brother in the Lord.

In the end, Father Joe never did make it back overseas. My wife accidentally found him at Our Lady of Peace Church when she stopped there to attend mass one Sunday in August, 1996. Subsequently, we joyously visited him several times. At our last luncheon together I fortuitously had my camera and took several now treasured pictures of the occasion. Father Joe died on Ash Wednesday, February 25, 1998. He was in his mid-eighties.

Even though there were only several days for church and family to attempt to notify the father's worldwide group of friends, central California's English and Vietnamese newspapers and radio and television stations sadly announced the loss and added wonderful, deserved tributes to Father Joe. His friends came to say good-bye from Texas, Iowa, and Los Angeles. Others sent flowers from Florida, Philadelphia, and other distant locations. The nightlong wake service, the following funeral mass, and final ceremonies at Our Lady of Peace, with the children's choir singing Father Joe's favorite songs, provided some small solace to those facing the sorrowful loss of this wonderful man.

Still, Father Joe's passing leaves an unfillable void in the multitude of lives he lovingly touched. Their final expression of gratitude and returned love was attested to by the estimated two thousand people who bade him farewell at his funeral.

Epilogue

At the end of *More Than a Soldier's War,* I wrote "The dark chapter [of America's abandonment of South Vietnam] ended when Hanoi's tanks smashed onto the grounds of the Presidential Palace in Saigon on April 30, 1975, only hours after the last Americans had been plucked by helicopter from the roof of the U.S. Embassy. In the end, all the suffering, hopes, sacrifices, all the blood and death had been for nothing."

That was the end for America, but it was just the beginning of another episode of suffering, blood, and death for hundreds of thousands of our South Vietnamese allies. True, it was all for nothing, but it was never *about* nothing. The effort in Vietnam was enjoined and suffered throughout for something that has been held precious by every race, ethnicity, and culture on this planet since the beginning of time. It was all about freedom.

Notwithstanding the expedient political motives and confined military tactics that drove unwise and costly decisions and actions at the White House and Pentagon, down at the bloodletting level in the jungles and rice paddies the motive for fighting was less convoluted, less complicated. Freedom was on the line.

Every Vietnamese I met during my seven years of service there who comprehended the true meaning and worth of freedom and the evil character of its Communist alternative fought to attain it, and, more important, were fully prepared to die in order to achieve it and pass it on to their children. Cynics have asked how could such people come to value and embrace the concept of freedom when it was unknown, even unthinkable, in previous centuries of their history and culture? The answer is that when almost one million northerners chose to flee south in 1954, they were consciously choosing freedom. The absence of freedom was clearly recognized when the people of the south experienced the brutal brand of Viet Cong "justice" that was imposed after sunset in scores of hamlets and villages. They expressed the will and desire to personally be involved in the attainment of it when 83 percent of eligible voters, countrywide, bravely disregarded the Viet Cong's threats and attempts to disrupt their country's first national election. In the end, after the fall of South Vietnam, hundreds of thousands, from every level of society, unhesitatingly chose to leave their beloved country in small, overcrowded, leaky boats and brave the unknown perils of the sea to escape to where freedom beckoned. One estimate claims that as many as sixty thousand drowned in the attempt.

From the American perspective, in retrospect, many confide that, given the cost so starkly etched into the wall of the Vietnam Memorial, the goal of achieving freedom for others in a distant, unfamiliar land, while perhaps a noble intention, was not worth the cost in human lives.

From the Vietnamese perspective, those who suffered before and after the fall of their country never doubted that the cause of freedom was just and warranted, particularly in view of the terrible amount of human treasure expended to grasp it. To this day, those who survived respect and deeply appreciate the efforts of Americans and other allies who stood beside them throughout that long, sad, and painful quest.

It seems most appropriate to quote here one of the many recorded expressions of mankind's eternal value of freedom. It was made by the English statesman John Stuart Mill (1806–1873).

> War is an ugly thing, but not the ugliest of things; the decayed and degraded state of moral and patriotic feeling which thinks that nothing is worth war is much worse.
>
> A man who has nothing for which he is willing to fight; nothing he cares about more than his own personal safety, is a miserable creature who has no chance of being free, unless made and kept so by the exertions of better men than himself.

Colonel Phuc expressed similar sentiments a hundred years later as chief of Dinh Tuong Province when he concluded a speech to the people of the province on National Day, November 1, 1967, in this manner:

> On the occasion of National Day this year, I ask all people of all levels to work and fight side by side to defeat our enemy and to rebuild a society applying equality and practicing charity.
>
> We must work with all our strength and contribute our blood and sweat in building a free nation, so we are not shamed in the eyes of our ancestors or seen as neglectful of our responsibility by our children and their children.

Index

EDWARD P. METZNER is a retired U.S. Army colonel who served seven years in Vietnam as an advisor to South Vietnamese military commanders from district and province levels to the Vietnamese Joint General Staff. He has told the story of his own experiences in *More Than A Soldier's War: Pacification in Vietnam,* also published by Texas A&M University Press. HUYNH VAN CHINH, TRAN VAN PHUC, and LE NGUYEN BINH were all colonels in the Army of Vietnam. All three now live in the United States.

ISBN 1-58544-129-5

9 781585 441297   90000